A Great Book OF American Songs

RUSSELL A. CLEMO

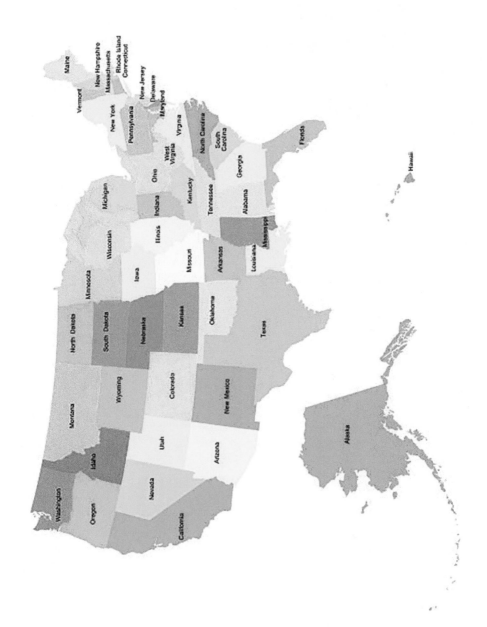

ABOUT THIS BOOK:

This book contains 120 written songs in 12 chapters without sheet music included. These collections of written songs are the creation of one author, Russell A. Clemo. This collection of songs spans many genres including Country music, Blues, Rock 'N' Roll, Bluegrass, Folk and New Alternative.

Printed in the United States of America

Publisher's Note

Ingram Spark Publishing Service & Subsidiary Lightning Source.
ISBN 979-8-218-30927-5

ACKNOWLEDGEMENTS:

To my parents Robert and Dee Clemo, and to my sibling's Jennie Clemo Fernandez, Christian Clemo, and Sarah Clemo Strand.

And to my extended family Doug Clemo, Daryl Duncan, Virginia Steinke, Shannon Watson, Jeff Steinke, Cyndi Thompson, Nadine Hanson, Mary Stuker, Barbara Skramstad, and Dave Duncan.

DEDICATION:

To my loving mother, Dee Clemo.

Chapter:

A Great Book of American Songs (I.)

Russell A. Clemo

INDEX

1. Country Boy Fight For Me
2. When Bombs Burst In Time
3. Tell me Brother What You Waiting For
4. In Times Of War
5. Comfort to a Man on a Cold Night
6. Making Love Is So Easy
7. We Got A Little Bit Of Wrangle
8. Firefly on That Mountain
9. The Dust Clouds Did Not Carry
10. I'm Still Going Crazy

By: Russell A. Clemo
Song Titled: **Country Boy Fight For Me**

Country Boy Fight For me
Be my eyes so I can see
Country boy land of the free
Country boy please fight for me
    Chorus

        Verse one:
I go away for a time
I fightin our wars
I come back home
Tell about the wars
Fighting for freedom
Even all the scores
Do it for stars and stripes
Do it for all the corps
Country boy fight for me
Country boy land of the free
I go away for a time
I fight for me
Home of the brave
Land of the free
I can see an eagle
He's watchen from the sky
Eagle help me see
Eagle doesn't tell me why

Country boy fight for me
Be my eyes so I can see
Country boy land of the free
Country boy please fight for me
    Chorus

Verse two:
You go away for a time
You fight in our wars
You come back home
Tell about the wars
Fighting for freedom
Even all the scores
Do it for stars and stripes
Do it for all the corps
Country boy fight for me
Country boy land of the free
You go away for a time
You fight for me
Home of the brave
Land of the free
You can see an eagle
He's watchen from the sky
Eagle helps him see
Eagle doesn't tell me why

County Boy fight for me
Be my eyes so I can see
Country boy land of the free
Country boy please fight for me
Chorus
....End song.

By: Russell A. Clemo
Song Titled: **When Bombs Burst In Time**

When Bombs Burst In Time
When you are fireworks
Let the sky be your light
Ya let it fill up your night
　　　Chorus

　　　Verse one:
We can go up baby
Ya fireworks go up
We can light up the sky
Ya we can get real high girl
I know it isn't natural
But baby we can fly up girl
You can take my hand up
We'll take to the sky baby
Ya we'll take to the sky
When bombs burst in time
When you are fireworks
Let the sky be your light
Ya let it fill up your night
All the beautiful people
They can fill up your night
Let the sky be your light
When we are fireworks

When Bombs Burst In Time
When you are fireworks
Let the sky be your light
Ya let it fill up your night
　　　Chorus

Verse two:
We can go up baby
Ya fireworks go up
We can light up the sky
Ya we can get real high girl
I know it isn't natural
But baby we can fly up
You can take my hand up
We'll take to the sky baby
Ya we'll take to the sky
When bombs burst in time
When you are fireworks
Let the sky be your light
Ya let it fill up your night
All the beautiful people
They can fill up your night
Let the sky be your light
When we are fireworks

When Bombs Burst in Time
When you are fireworks
Let the sky be your light
Ya let it fill up your night
        Chorus .
                ....End song

By: Russell A. Clemo
Song Titled: **Tell me Brother What You Waiting For**

Tell Me Brother What You Waiting For
Tell me what the future has in store
How can we get any further
Tell me what are you waiting for
      Chorus

      Verse one:
Your hands are yours
Your hands are mine
Together we can read
We can read that sign
We're waiting together
Don't make me wait forever
Snow on a mountain
When it melts it's runnen
Running wild and free
Come to me in that valley
Water just for me
Tell me brother what you waiting for
When it fills the lakes and streams
Feed this land and some dreams
That builds a place for me
You tryen to get a little further
Tell me what you waiting for
Plant some new seeds
Take all of your things to store
Make it with your hands
Together we can make much more
You can find you a wife
Make yourself a beautiful life
Make for you a beautiful life

Tell me brother what you waiting for
Tell me what the future has in store
How can we get any further
Tell me what are you waiting for
      Chorus

      Verse two:
Your hands are yours
Your hands are mine
Together we can read
We can read that sign
We're waiting together
Don't make me wait forever
Snow on a mountain
When it melts it's runnen
Running wild and free
Come to me in that valley
Water just for me
Tell me brother what you waiting for
When it fills the lakes and streams
Feed this land and some dreams
That builds a place for me
You tryen to get a little further
Tell me what you waiting for
Plant some new seeds
Take all of your things to store
Make it with your hands
Together we can make much more
You can find you a wife
Make yourself a beautiful life
Make for you a beautiful life

Tell me brother what you waiting for
Tell me what the future has in store
How can we get any further
Tell me what are you waiting for.
      Chorus
         ....End song

 By: Russell A. Clemo
Song Titled: **In Times Of War**

In times of war
I call from over seas
I want to be with you baby
God return me please
     Chorus

     Verse one:
Shells rain from the sky
How many soldiers out here
How many gonna die
Everybody out here
Little children wonder why
They are running around over here
That makes a soldier wonder why
A soldier serving over here
I'm a soldier till I die
Shells raining from the sky
My friends are dien over here
I've looked evil in it's eye
We are still trying over here
I wanna hear a helicopter in the sky
Too many soldiers over here
Honey we ain't gonna die
Finally I can hear it now

In times of war
I call from over seas
I want to be with you baby
God return me please
     Chorus

Verse two:
Shells rain from the sky
How many soldiers out here
How many gonna die
Everybody out here
Little children wonder why
They are running around over here
That makes a soldier wonder why
A soldier serving over here
I'm a soldier till I die
Shells raining from the sky
My friends are dien over here
I've looked evil in it's eye
We are still trying over here
I wanna hear a helicopter in the sky
Too many soldiers over here
Honey we ain't gonna die
Finally I can hear it now

In times of war
I call from over seas
I wanna be with you baby
God return me please
        Chorus
            ....End song

By: Russell A. Clemo
Song Titled: **Comfort to a Man on a Cold Night**

Comfort to a man on a cold night
Preparations made outside
Staring at a campfires light
Not looking through something's missing
I don't need it if it's broken
        Chorus

        Verse one:
Helped now by the wind
Stoke the fire again
Maken it burn brighter
Tranquil contrast to the unchecked
Something more while I reflect
Something comen over me
Maken new plans remenicen
Remenicen on some history
Whenever I'm in the city
I know those woods are missing me
Long conversations to a fires light
Let warmth hug me close
Let us make the most
My campfire dreamen
Baby please talk to me
Staren at a campfires light
Sometimes just like that
I like it when I'm all alone
Looken up at the stars
Someday I know they'll be calling me home
But until then Baby
Ya until then Baby
I'll be maken plans like this
Ya I'll be maken plans like this

Comfort to a man on a cold night
Preparations made outside

Staren at a campfires light
Not looking through something missing
I don't need it if it's broken
    Chorus

        Verse two:
I said oh my-goodness me
What has been given
what keeps given to me
Reasons to be thankful for
I know I can see
What are these woods doin to me
Wood burnen in that campfire
Cut from the same water same stone
Everytime I find it hard to leave
Every other weekend I call it home
I know those woods are missing me
Long conversations to a fires light
I might take me a woman
Need her warmth to hug me close
By my campfire dreaming
We can enjoy a long silence
While both of us are dreaming
Maybe all we hear is silence
But the love holds me close
Her and me making the most
Let's watch the sun as it's rising
Put some coffee on
Watch the woods start to liven
All night them woods that campfire livened

Comfort to a man on a cold night
Preperations made outside
Staren at a campfires light
Not looking through something missing
I don't need it if it's broken
    Chorus
        ....End song

By: Russell A. Clemo
Song Titled: **Making Love Is So Easy**

Making love is so easy
Ya so let's take it slow
With just a little bit of gas baby
Ya I know just where to go
      Chorus

      Verse one:
Taken a slow drive honey
Driven down memory lane
Got one hand on you baby
I ain't worried about a thing
One hand on the steering wheel
We'll see what love brings
Quiet drives and long talks now
We do all of this hand in hand
So go on and take my hand now
Making love is so easy
Ya so let's take it slow
With just a little bit of gas baby
Ya I know just where to go
Somewhere on a two lane highway
In the rain or in the snow
Ya we don't mind sunshine baby
Man we stay ready to go
Oh baby now turn on that radio

Making love is so easy
Ya so let's take it slow
With just a little bit of gas baby
Ya I know just where to go
      Chorus

Verse two:
We'll make that slow drive honey
Driving down memory lane
Still got one hand on you baby
No you ain't worried about a thing
Still got a hand on the steering wheel
Ya we'll see what love brings
Quiet drives and long talks now
We do all of this hand in hand
So go on and take my hand now
Making love is so easy
Ya so let's take it slow
With just a little bit of gas baby
Ya I know just where to go
Somewhere on a two lane highway
In the rain or in the snow
No we don't mind sunshine baby
Man we stay ready to go
Oh now baby turn on that radio

Making love is so easy
Ya so let's take it slow
With just a little bit of gas baby
Ya I know just where to go
        Chorus
                ....End song

By: Russell A. Clemo
Song Titled: **We Got A Little Bit Of Wrangle**

We Got A Little Bit Of Wrangle
We got a little bit of rope & ride
We got a little bit of country twang
That's how we do it on our side
            Chorus

        Verse one:
Take my hand little darlin
You can wear my cowboy hat
I'll even let you drive my truck
Tell me what you think about that
Its early in the morning baby
Or bonfire sitting on a tailgate
It's on all the time with me darlin
You know I can barely wait
Ya you can barely wait
We got a little bit of wrangle
We got a little bit of rope & ride
We got a little bit of country twang
That's how we do it on our side
I'll always make time for you
My heart can barely wait
Baby you can watch it dance for you
Watch my heart dance inside it's fate

We got a little bit of wrangle
We got a little bit of rope & ride
We got a little bit of country twang
That's how we do it on our side
            Chorus

Verse two:
When I take your hand little darlin
When you wear my cowboy hat
I love when you drive my truck
Tell me what you think about that
Is it early in the morning baby
Or bonfire sitting on a tailgate
You're on all the time honey
You know I can barely wait
Ya you can barely wait
We got a little bit of wrangle
We got a little bit of rope & ride
We got a little bit of country twang
That's how we do it on our side
I know you'll always make time for me
My heart it can barely wait
baby watch it dance for you
My heart dancen inside it's fate

We got a little bit of wrangle
We got a little bit of rope & ride
We got a little bit of country twang
That's how we do it on our side
Chorus
....End song

By: Russell A. Clemo
Song Titled: **Firefly on That Mountain**

Firefly on that mountain
Firefly in a dream
Firefly on that water
Firefly on a stream
You come to me in a dream
        Chorus

        Verse one:
Firefly out there chasen
Chase the honey bee
You take to water
You're just like me
I can feel you flyen
You're flyen next to me
I can see you're looken
Take me steadily
Your colors are brilliant
Show me in the light
New and ancient in the light
How can a dream feel so right
Firefly out there chasen
You can set me free
You're out there flyen
Chase the honey bee
Next time I go to sleep
Come and follow me
I'll be there waiting
I know I will see
So vivid in creation
I know it has to be
Intimate in creation
I know it has to be

Firefly on that mountain
Firefly in a dream

Firefly on that water
Firefly on a stream
You come to me in a dream
        Chorus

        Verse two:
Firefly out there chasen
Chase the honey bee
You take to water
You're just like me
I can feel you flyen
You're flyen next to me
I can see you're looken
Take me steadily
Your colors are brilliant
Show me in the light
New and ancient in the light
How can a dream feel so right
Firefly out there chasen
You can set me free
You're out there flyen
Chase the honey bee
Next time I go to sleep
Come and follow me
I'll be there waiting
I know I will see
So vivid in creation
I know it has to be
Intimate in creation
I know it has to be

Firefly on that mountain
Firefly in a dream
Firefly on that water
Firefly on a stream
You come to me in a dream
        Chorus
                ....End song

By: Russell A. Clemo
Song Titled: **The Dust Clouds Did Not Carry**

The dust clouds did not carry
They didn't carry this far
What lies contained inside
How could it carry this far
      Chorus

      Verse one:
I can see it on the wind
My best friend he can see it to
We can see it twinned
When that storm is coming
When the war drums are drumming
If it wasn't before peace
We can see a peace that's coming
Rain drops in that water
Raining down on me
Rain drops in that water
Raining down on you
Ya you can feel it too
Out in the high desert
In a valley of treasures
We can see stormy weather
It rolls in from a mile away
That gives us half the day
I'm looken up at the sky

The dust clouds did not carry
They didn't carry this far
What lies contained inside
How could it carry this far
      Chorus

Verse two:
When I can't see it
I can't see it on the wind
When I'm inside of that storm
I can feel it all around
Feel it like a swarm
That's what makes me cold
That's what makes me warm
I feel it before some rain
Seeing water in my pain
Is there a storm coming
You see a storm coming
Somewhere in that dust cloud
You tell me right as rain
Tell me what is coming
See it in that dust cloud
It rolls in from a mile away
That gives us half the day
I'm looking up at the sky

The dust clouds did not carry
They didn't carry this far
What lies contained inside
How could it carry this far
    Chorus
        ....End song

By: Russell A. Clemo
Song Titled: **I'm Still Going Crazy**

I'm still going crazy
That'll take me to
Take me to Tennessee baby
Gotta keep going just for you
        Chorus

        Verse one::
I swear I'm leaving town now
When I leave you'll come to
I've gotta chase my dreams
In my dreams I need you
Let's take a chance honey
Country music keeps me true
You know this drives me crazy
Baby I'm gonna dance with you
We're two wild horses baby
Even when I'm running back to you
I guess I can leave without you honey
But I don't think that I need to
Your chasing dreams with me baby
Two mustangs running without a clue
I have so much love for you honey
That's why I'm doing this dance with you
Let's do this like wild horses baby
Taken off across this country too

I'm still going crazy
That'll take me to
Take me to Tennessee baby
Gotta keep going just for you
        Chorus

Verse two::
You swear your leaving town now
When I leave you'll come to
Baby's coming to chase my dreams
In my dreams I need you
Thanks for taking that chance honey
Country music keeps me true
Baby this life's driving me crazy
Ya and I'm gonna dance with you
We're two wild horses honey
Even when I'm running back to you
I can leave without you baby
But I don't think that I need to
Chasing dreams with you honey
Ya two mustangs without a clue
Baby all this love is for you
That's why I'm doing this dance its true
Let's do this like wild horses baby
Taken off across this country too

I'm still going crazy
That'll take me to
Take me to Tennessee baby
Gotta keep going just for you
            Chorus
                    ....End song

Chapter:

A Great Book of American Songs (II.)

Russell A. Clemo

INDEX

1. Sometimes You're Looken Back at Me
2. A Big Sky Country Keeps Me Waiten
3. How Can We Be Free
4. My Addiction and Some Sin
5. He's Your Country Star Boy
6. Ever Since That Spark
7. You Can Almost Feel The Heat
8. Good Morning To You
9. Need Beauty In Some Time
10. I'm Thinking About A Country Christmas

By: Russell A. Clemo
Song Titled: **Sometimes You're Looken Back at Me**

Sometimes you're looken back at me
Looken at me in the mirror
You tell me to be that man
The one I was meant to be
        Chorus

        Verse one:
I miss you daddy
I miss your smile
Miss when you'd talk to me
every once in awhile
every day your memory
I can see inside my smile
That's you inside of me
It carries me a country mile
Sometimes you're looken back at me
Looken at me in the mirror
You tell me to be that man
The one I was meant to be
What lies between us
I'm a part of that history
I promise not to walk away
I'll stand right by your side
You can still see through me
Inside it's my family pride.

Sometimes you're looken back at me
Looken at me in the mirror
You tell me to be that man
The one I was meant to be
        Chorus

Verse two:
I miss you daddy
I miss your smile
One day when I have a son
I know I'll see your smile
every day your memory
I can see inside his smile
That's you inside of him
It'll carry me a country mile
Sometimes you're looken back at me
Looken at me in the mirror
You tell me to be that man
The one I was meant to be
What lies between us
I'm a part of that history
I promise not to walk away
I'll stand right by your side
You can still see through me
Inside it's my family pride.

Sometimes you're looken back at me
Looken at me in the mirror
You tell me to be that man
The one I was meant to be
        Chorus
                ....End song

By: Russell A. Clemo
Song Titled: **A Big Sky Country Keeps Me Waiten**

A Big Sky Country Keeps Me Waiten
Hold it all together and help me now
You hold it all together help me now
I can feel it slipping away
          Chorus

          Verse one:
A beacon of hope
There's hope in the darkness
I can search for a light
Don't want to search here forever
I have a friend in the dark
In the path of lesser darkness
My friend finds that light
With just a moment to recognize
I'm steady on my horse
While he's steady on that course
Now I know I realise
You can take on the mud
Come another rush of water
But it won't wash away
It'll hold you here today
We can bring it all home
I'm ready to bring it all home
What keeps us here waiting

A Big Sky Country Keeps Me Waiten
Hold it all together and help me now
You hold it all together help me now
I can feel it slipping away
          Chorus

Verse two:
A beacon of hope
There's hope in the darkness
I can search for a light
Don't want to search here forever
God watch me on that horse
Hold me steady on my course
Through snowy mountains and high desert
With just a moment to recognize
When the mud is coming
When the rain is coming
While I'm looking up at the stars
I can feel another force
Riding on a Montana horse
Looking at the Yellowstone River
Horse take me down that river
We can bring it all home
I'm ready to bring it all home
What keeps us here waiting

A Big Sky Country Keeps Me Waiten
Hold it all together and help me now
You hold it all together help me now
I can feel it slipping away
Chorus
....End song

By: Russell A. Clemo
Song Titled: **How Can We Be Free**

How Can We Be Free
Eyes so I can see
You hear just for me
Will us to be free
      Chorus

      Verse one:
Angel inside I'm free
Demon inside is killing me
What does it take to be
Lock that door carefully
I didn't want to give away
Give away my key
Give it away for me
What makes us sober
What makes this some disorder
Let a stranger come for me
Let the stranger set us free
Both you and me now
His questions with her own
I can see in between
See inside a broken dream
See inside of that line
Walking here in time
Don't take that away

How Can We Be Free
Eyes so I can see
You hear just for me
Will us to be free
      Chorus

Verse two:
Wild horse inside of me
Wild horses running free
Open range on some land
Or maybe in that city
Wherever it was planned
What does it take to be
What does it mean to you
You gonna tell me please
Wait I didn't ask you
Don't tell us please
Tell me what's the use
Baby tell me what's the use
I can see a free world
One free without destruction
Ya unity and a function
I can see brothers
brothers inside they're free
We can write some history

How Can We Be Free
Eyes so I can see
You hear just for me
Will us to be free
Chorus
....End song

By: Russell A. Clemo
Song Titled: **My Addiction and Some Sin**

My addiction and some sin
The water that I'm dancen in
What's underneath my skin
Tell me is it in your plan
I just want to be an honest man
      Chorus

      Verse one:
What if I walked away
Just walked away from it all
What if I learned to stumble
What if I learned to crawl
If I was an honest man
I could give it all
A drink for my affliction
Some whiskey for my affliction
I drowned in the drink
You can lead this horse to water
You can make him drink
Who needs the water
Tell me what you think
Starin at a valley of horses
Come on tell me what you think
what if I walked away
Just walked away from it all
How far do I need to fall
Thinken about the good life
That's what I'm telling you
I'm drinking some whiskey
I'm still liven in sin
While I'm still looking up above
I'm still looking up above

My addiction and some sin
The water that I'm dancen in

What's underneath my skin
Tell me is it in your plan
I just want to be an honest man
        Chorus

        Verse two:
What if I walked away
Leave my broken dreams
Maybe start somewhere new
Still have some good dreams
Good dreams I'll share with you
What's underneath of my skin
Watch and see what I do
Whiskey knows I need a friend
Me and whiskey singen for two
Listen to the guitar
Tell me is it in your plan
If I was an honest man
I'm still liven in sin
Ya drinken from a bottle
Pull up a chair my friend
You and I can share this bottle
Maybe a drink for your affliction
Feel it all fall away
Maybe a drink for the good life
I'll let you tell me the way
Ya we've got all afternoon
We can do this all day
While I'm still looking up above
I'm still looking up above

My addiction and some sin
The water that I'm dancen in
What's underneath my skin
Tell me is it in your plan
I just want to be an honest man
        Chorus
                ....End song

By: Russell A. Clemo
Song Titled: **He's Your Country Star Boy**

He's your country star boy
Ya in a lifted truck now
He's a young and country boy
Ride in his lifted truck now
      Chorus

      Verse one:
Windows down it's gettin hotter
Still riding around town
Truck is sitten up real high
Listen to my music sound
Hear the subwoofers playing
Ya let everything else drowned
Wind blowing through the cab
Ain't lost don't need to be found
Budlight and do a little dab
He's your country star boy
Ya in a lifted truck now
He's a young and country boy
Ride in his lifted truck now
Windows down riding around town
Pretty girls riding with him baby
I'm your country star boy
Drive you country star crazy
I'll drive you all around town

He's your country star boy
Ya in a lifted truck now
He's a young and country boy
Ride in his lifted truck now
      Chorus

Verse two:
Windows down it's gettin hotter
Do you wanna ride with me now
Passenger seat sitten up real high
Viben to that music sound
Baby if you ride it's do or die
Ya let everything else drowned
Wind blowing through the cab
Wind blowing through the town
Ain't lost don't need to be found
He's your country star boy
In a lifted truck now
He's a young and country boy
Ride in his lifted truck now
Windows down riding around town
Pretty girls riding with him baby
I'm your country star boy
Drive you country star crazy
I'll drive you all around town

He's your country star boy
Ya in a lifted truck now
He's a young and country boy
Ride in his lifted truck now
Chorus
....End song

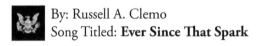 By: Russell A. Clemo
Song Titled: **Ever Since That Spark**

Ever since that spark
I knew she was the one
My mind exploding with 21 guns
Burning bright hot like the sun
        Chorus

        Verse one:
I keep thinking of ways
Ways to tell her I love you
She's that beautiful girl
So beautiful and true
You can see diamonds
The diamonds in her eyes
They sparkle really blue
Looking at a blue horizon
Somewhere she can liven
Lots of blue water
You and me let's dive In
We can swim eight miles out
With those diamonds in your eyes
It's just you and me
We can do anything
I'll buy you a diamond ring
Have a big wedding chapel
We'll have a rock star sing

Ever since that spark
I knew she was the one
My mind exploding with 21 guns
Burning bright hot like the sun
        Chorus

Verse two:
I keep thinking of ways
Ways to tell her I love you
She's that beautiful girl
So beautiful and true
Somewhere out there baby
Somewhere on a beach
Walk along the beach
With our toes in the sand
We can dance happily
We'll enjoy the sunny weather
Have some umbrella drinks
Lots of rum and tequila
Serve you a morning margarita
Or early morning consuela
We can do anything
I'll buy you a diamond ring
Have a big wedding chapel
We'll have a rock star sing

Ever since that spark
I knew she was the one
My mind exploding with 21 guns
Burning bright hot like the sun
Chorus
....End song

By: Russell A. Clemo
Song Titled: **You Can Almost Feel The Heat**

You can almost feel the heat
Its hot like 4th of July
Everyday of summer
Sweet like mom's apple pie
         Chorus

         Verse one:
Sweetest girl look me in my eye
She tell me every little truth
She tell me every little lie
First time I ever saw her
She made me want to cry
Gets her looks from her mama
First look I almost died
With all her charms from her daddy
I told her how I feel inside
Looken deeper into some mountains
On the high desert side
Tryen to see what it will take
Parked out by a lake
Settling for a long eventful afternoon
I need the smell of her perfume
Every long eventful afternoon
She loves to sweep me off of my feet
Looking deeper into those mountains

You can almost feel the heat
Its hot like 4th of July
Everyday of summer
Sweet like mom's apple pie
         Chorus

Verse two:
Sweetest girl look me in my eye
She tell me every little truth
She tell me every little lie
First time I ever saw her
She made me want to cry
Gets her looks from her mama
First look I almost died
With all her charms from her daddy
I told her how I feel inside
Looken deeper into some mountains
On the high desert side
Tryen to see what it will take
Parked out by a lake
Settling for a long eventful afternoon
I need the smell of her perfume
Every long eventful afternoon
She loves to sweep me off of my feet
Looking deeper into those mountains

....End song

By: Russell A. Clemo
Song Titled: **Good Morning To You**

Good morning to you
So beautiful and true
Thinking about mom
I know how much
How much that I love you
    Chorus

    Verse one:
Sunshine and some breeze
Thinking on an afternoon
You and me shooting the breeze
I can talk to you for hours
While looking out at some trees
Tell me what you're thinking
It always puts me at ease
We're sharing hearts together
I wish time would freeze
The smell of honey suckle
There's feathered birds and honey bees
You're a part of that good life
Another shot of the good life please
Love that your heart brings
Ya that's when my heart sings
Let God smile down on us
It will last forever
In God we trust

Good morning to you
So beautiful and true
Thinking about mom
I know how much
How much that I love you
    Chorus

Verse two:
Sunshine and some breeze
Thinking on an afternoon
You and me shooting the breeze
I can talk to you for hours
While looking out at some trees
Tell me what you're thinking
It always puts me at ease
We're sharing hearts together
I wish time would freeze
The smell of honey suckle
There's feathered birds and honey bees
You're a part of that good life
Another shot of the good life please
Love that your heart brings
Ya that's when my heart sings
Let God smile down on us
It will last forever
In God we trust
....End song

By: Russell A. Clemo
Song Titled: **Need Beauty In Some Time**

Need Beauty In Some Time
Think I'll sit here for a time
Let everything run across my mind
As everything runs across your mind
        Chorus

        Verse one:
Sitting with my legs dangling
I'm dangled over a cliff
Looking out at a river
This is the way I live
When I can't shake a feeling
Something has got to give
I wish my emotions weren't so
But they get the best of me
Everywhere that I go darling
Need beauty in some time
I'm young at heart
Need to calm my mind
Need to settle down
There's no need to rewind
That's what is good for me
I'll let someone else worry
Don't need to let it worry me
I've got love and good family

Need Beauty In Some Time
Think I'll sit here for a time
Let everything run across my mind
As everything runs across your mind
        Chorus

Verse two:
Sitting with my legs dangling
I'm dangled over a cliff
Looking out at a river
This is the way I live
When I can't shake a feeling
Something has got to give
I wish my emotions weren't so
But they get the best of me
Everywhere that I go darling
Need beauty in some time
I'm young at heart
Need to calm my mind
Need to settle down
There's no need to rewind
That's what is good for me
I'll let someone else worry
Don't need to let it worry me
I've got love and good family

....End song

By: Russell A. Clemo
Song Titled: **I'm Thinking About A Country Christmas**

I'm thinking about a country Christmas
America and a lot of snow
Everybody enjoying their Christmas
You better find some mistletoe
    Chorus

    Verse one:
If your slow dancing baby
With fires all a glow
If you feel it inside honey
Then maybe you do know
You can dance with me
We do it around a Christmas tree
Have some eggnog ready to go
We still need one more dance
Then we'll find some mistletoe
I'm thinking about a country Christmas
That's what you were thinking too
This season is about love
Ya so there is plenty for you
Let me get closer now baby
There will be just enough for two
I'm feelin love for you and Christmas baby
Save me another slow dance with you
This year its all about you

I'm thinking about a country Christmas
America and a lot of snow
Everybody enjoying their Christmas
You better find some mistletoe
    Chorus

Verse two:
If I'm slow dancin baby
With fires all a glow
If you feel it honey
I already know you know
Dance with me little baby
We do it around a Christmas tree
Rum and eggnog ready to go
We need one more dance baby
You need some mistletoe
This is a country Christmas
That's what you were thinking too
This season's about the love
There is plenty for you
We're getten closer now baby
Ya just enough for two
I'm about you and Christmas baby
Another slow dance with you
This year its all about you

I'm thinking about a country Christmas
America and a lot of snow
Everybody enjoying their Christmas
You better find some mistletoe
        Chorus
                ....End song

CHAPTER:

A Great Book of American Songs (III.)

Russell A. Clemo

INDEX

1. I Wanna Sing Like Willie Nelson
2. I Love Your Imperfections
3. Snow on the Rocky Mountains
4. Sitting Underneath Some City Lights
5. Your Pretty Hazel Eyes
6. A Piece of Colorado in Arizona
7. A Cowboy In The Echoes
8. She Says She Hasn't Made Up Her Mind
9. A Cowboy On The Pacific Trail
10. Kootenai Valley On That Yaak River

By: Russell A. Clemo
Song Titled: **I Wanna Sing Like Willie Nelson**

I Wanna Sing Like Willie Nelson
I wanna see the country side
Down home country boy
Traveling the country side
Write my songs like that
How do I live a life like that
      Chorus

      Verse one:
See the lights on the interstate
In another town another stage
I'm getting on the bus again
I'm traveling on the road
Ya the road is an old friend
I bring my family with me
Let them play in my band
See the world every day
It's just how I planned
Singin to a country crowd
A country boy will play it loud
Live a life like that
Ya I wanna sing like Willie Nelson
I wanna see the country side
Wear a hole in my six-string
Wanna wear it with pride
Ya playin my guitar for you
I play it every night

I Wanna Sing Like Willie Nelson
I wanna see the country side
Down home country boy
Traveling the country side
Write my songs like that
How do I live a life like that
      Chorus

Verse two:
See the lights on the interstate
In another town another stage
I'm getting on the bus again
I'm traveling on the road
Ya the road is an old friend
I bring my family with me
Let them play in my band
See the world every day
It's just how I planned
Singin to a country crowd
A country boy will play it loud
Live a life like that
Ya I wanna sing like Willie Nelson
I wanna see the country side
Wear a hole in my six-string
Wanna wear it with pride
Ya playin my guitar for you
I play it every night

I Wanna Sing Like Willie Nelson
I wanna see the country side
Down home country boy
Traveling the country side
Write my songs like that
How do I live a life like that
Chorus
....End song

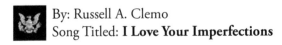 By: Russell A. Clemo
Song Titled: **I Love Your Imperfections**

I Love Your Imperfections
When I can see those things
They're perfect reflections
All of the unseen
    Chorus

    Verse one:
What makes you real to me
What makes you real to you
It's okay if it hurts a little
I'll help you through it all
We'll get there together
We can get through it all
If it isn't your crooked smile
You're obsessing over things
Have another glass of wine
Forget about those things
If it isn't about family
Love our family brings
I won't let it in your heart
I'll make sure your heart sings
I love your crooked smile
The way you're obsessing over things
Have another glass of wine
I'll help you forget about those things.

I Love Your Imperfections
When I can see those things
They're perfect reflections
All of the unseen
    Chorus

Verse two:
What makes you real to me
What makes you real to you
It's okay if it hurts a little
I'll help you through it all
We'll get there together
We can get through it all
If it isn't your crooked smile
You're obsessing over things
Have another glass of wine
Forget about those things
If it isn't about family
Love our family brings
I won't let it in your heart
I'll make sure your heart sings
I love your crooked smile
The way you're obsessing over things
Have another glass of wine
I'll help you forget about those things.

I Love Your Imperfections
When I can see those things
They're perfect reflections
All of the unseen
Chorus
....End song

By: Russell A. Clemo
Song Titled: **Snow on the Rocky Mountains**

Snow on the Rocky Mountains
I can see from my aeroplane
Snow on those mountains
I'm landing in Colorado again
      Chorus

      Verse one:
It's three minutes after six
I'm just touched down
Call ahead to an old friend
Told her I'll be around
We'll have dinner one night
You can show me around
I'd like to see your ranch
At last I'm ready
It's been a while now
You and me been steady
I'm ready you say when
I'm landing in Colorado again
Those Rocky Mountains visit me
Visit me in my dreams
That's when I see you
I think I know what that means
I brought you rubies and pearls
You deserve the finer things
I'm hoping you'll accept me
Because I think I'm ready to stay
I wanna be here for you darlin
Each and every day
I'm ready you say when
Please tell me to stay.

Snow on the Rocky Mountains
I can see from my aeroplane
Snow on those mountains
I'm landing in Colorado again
        Chorus

        Verse two:
One trip around the world
I leave to come back again
That's when I call ahead
Call ahead to an old friend
Tell her that I'm comin home
I'm ready you say when
You finally asked me to stay
Now I'm comin back to you again
I brought you a diamond this time
You deserve the finer things
I hope you like diamond rings
I'm landing in Colorado again
Those Rocky Mountains visit me
Visit me in my dreams
That's when I see you
I think I know what that means
I'm gonna play my guitar for you
Show you how this cowboy sings
That's how I'll ask to marry you
Together we'll see what the future brings
I wanna be here for you darlin
Each and every day
I'm ready you say when
Please tell me to stay

Snow on the Rocky Mountains
I can see from my aeroplane
Snow on those mountains
I'm landing in Colorado again
        Chorus
                ....End song

By: Russell A. Clemo
Song Titled: **Sitting Underneath Some City Lights**

Sitting Underneath Some City Lights
I love those city lights
I know their not just for me
I know their not just for me
        Chorus

        Verse one:
While I'm underneath those city lights
I'm underneath of a spell
When I'm all alone
I can feel their spell
Bright city lights talk to me
Tell me about your life
Tell me your history
I'll tell you about my life
Won't leave out the mystery
We can go on like that
Until I have to leave
Until you're missing me
I'm underneath those city lights
Why is my life this way
They're always pulling me
Which way to go now
Tell which way to see
Tell me how I should move forward
Who am I going to be
I can feel them now
I know they're not just for me
Tell me you can feel them too
I know they're not just for me
Do they talk to you

Sitting Underneath Some City Lights
I love those city lights
I know their not just for me
I know their not just for me
        Chorus

        Verse two:
I'm underneath those city lights
I can feel in a spell
When I'm all alone
I can feel their spell
Come to me in a dream
When I'm feeling sleepy
Walking sleepy in a dream
If you could tell me your life
Tell me your history
Only tell me about the good life
Just leave out the mystery
I can go on like that
Until you're missing me
I'm underneath those city lights
Why is my life this way
They're always pulling me
Which way to go now
Tell me which way to see
Tell me how I should move forward
Who am I going to be
I can feel them now
I know they're not just for me
Tell me can you feel them too
I know they're not just for me

Sitting Underneath Some City Lights
I love those city lights
I know their not just for me
I know their not just for me
        Chorus
                ….End song

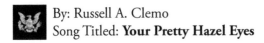 By: Russell A. Clemo
Song Titled: **Your Pretty Hazel Eyes**

Your Pretty Hazel Eyes
With some candle lights
Your love so inviting to me
You know what you mean to me
          Chorus

        Verse one:
Some woods on a lake
When you need that break
Leave the city life
Ripple in the wake
Another ripple in time
Your heart is yours
Your heart is mine
It ain't ever easy
While it ain't hard to find
Ya what you give to me
I give to you
What we hold is sacred
My heart is true
That's my promise to you
My every living day
That's what holds us here
Love always finds a way
Loven in times like this

Your Pretty Hazel Eyes
With some candle lights
Your love so inviting to me
You know what you mean to me
          Chorus

Verse two:
Some woods on a lake
When you need that break
Leave the city life
Ripple in the wake
Another ripple in time
Your heart is yours
Your heart is mine
It ain't ever easy
While it ain't hard to find
Ya what you give to me
I give to you
What we hold is sacred
My heart is true
That's my promise to you
My every living day
That's what holds us here
Love always finds a way
Loven in times like this

....End song

By: Russell A. Clemo
Song Titled: **A Piece of Colorado in Arizona**

A Piece of Colorado in Arizona
I'm going on a canyon ride
Camping in a canyon side
There's a little piece of Colorado
A Piece of Colorado in Arizona
      Chorus

      Verse one:
There's dust in the sky
There's dust in my eyes
There's purples pinks and blues
I can see brilliant colors
They all look so true
Floating down that river
It's the Colorado blue
I'm somewhere down in Arizona
I don't need to tell you
Paradise is on that river
Ya paradise it's so true
I'm going on a canyon ride
Camping in a canyon side
Cowboy on a cowboy ride
See so deep inside you'll see
Take a look inside you'll see
That dust in the sky
There's purples pinks and blues

A Piece of Colorado in Arizona
I'm going on a canyon ride
Camping in a canyon side
There's a little piece of Colorado
A Piece of Colorado in Arizona
      Chorus

Verse two:
There's dust in the sky
There's dust in my eyes
There's purples pinks and blues
I can see brilliant colors
We make our campfire for the night
Campfire with a campfire's light
Outside I feel a canyon's ghost
Spirit with us making the most
Embrace all the stars in the sky
Embrace the love it feels so right
Star child come dance with me
The fire's light makes me feel so free
Camping in a canyon side
Cowboy on a cowboy ride
See so deep inside you'll see
Take a look inside you'll see
That dust in the sky
There's purples pinks and blues

....End song

By: Russell A. Clemo
Song Titled: **A Cowboy In The Echoes**

A Cowboy In The Echoes
Inside I can feel you too
Someone tell me what to do
A cowboy in the echoes
      Chorus

      Verse one:
I know what you're thinking
When you tell me what to do
I know which way I'm going
Someone tell me what to do
I can see in the silence
I can see when it echoes
Together we can feel it voice
Together we're as one
Tell me what is real
We're all under the sun
We all need someone
Who is man's best friend
I'm trying to feel it under the sun
Tell me what is real
Ya you tell me what is real
We're all looken at a blue horizon
These aren't empty skies that liven
I can feel inside the echoes

A Cowboy In The Echoes
Inside I can feel you too
Someone tell me what to do
A cowboy in the echoes
      Chorus

Verse two:
I know what you're thinking
When you tell me what to do
I know which way I'm going
Someone tell me what to do
I can see in the silence
I can see when it echoes
Together we can feel it voice
Together we're as one
Tell me what is real
We're all under the sun
We all need someone
Who is man's best friend
I'm trying to feel it under the sun
Tell me what is real
Ya you tell me what is real
We're all looken at a blue horizon
These aren't empty skies that liven
I can feel inside the echoes

A Cowboy In The Echoes
Inside I can feel you too
Someone tell me what to do
A cowboy in the echoes
        Chorus
                ....End song

By: Russell A. Clemo
Song Titled: **She Says She Hasn't Made Up Her Mind**

She Says She Hasn't Made Up Her Mind
Every time that she walks away
I think it's the very last time
She comes back just to walk away
　　　Chorus

　　　Verse one:
She's so in love with me
I take her back a million times
Her love takes me away
She can read between the lines
She's walken all over me
She knows I need her story lines
Want her to have a child with me
I forgive her a million times
All she has to do is smile for me
Come on baby read the signs
I tell her make a life with me
She says she hasn't made up her mind
But I know it's in her mind
Taking steps so she can see
The clues they aren't hard to find
While she's walken all over me
I show her how it was designed
Now I can't let her walk away

She Says She Hasn't Made Up Her Mind
Every time that she walks away
I think it's the very last time
She comes back just to walk away
　　　Chorus

Verse two:
I'm so in love with her
She'll come back to me a million times
Her love takes me away
We finally had a daughter
She comes back just to walk away
She knows I need her story lines
She's just like her mama
I forgive her a million times
All she has to do is smile for me
Come on baby read the signs
I tell her make a life with me
She says she hasn't made up her mind.
But I know it's in her mind
Taking steps so she can see
The clues they aren't hard to find
While she's walken all over me
I show her how it was designed
Now I can't let her walk away

She Says She Hasn't Made Up Her Mind
Every time that she walks away
I think it's the very last time
She comes back just to walk away
Chorus
....End song

By: Russell A. Clemo
Song Titled: **A Cowboy On The Pacific Trail**

A Cowboy On The Pacific Trail
With supplies and gear on my back
With the sweat on my brow
I can see the Pacific Trail like that
      Chorus

      Verse one:
Hiking into some trees
Just me and them honey bees
With 75 pounds of gear on my back
Ya gonna see the country just like that
I know it's just like that
If it's rain snow or shine
So intimate it is to me
All of them woods and coastline
This wilderness is a part of me
This is my home away from home
Hiking into some wilderness
If I can't find my way back home
The sweat on my brow fallen down
The 75 pounds of gear on my back
Eagle please don't fail me now
Push just one more bend in that trek
With the sweat on my brow
I can see the Pacific Trail like that

A Cowboy On The Pacific Trail
With supplies and gear on my back
With the sweat on my brow
I can see the Pacific Trail like that
      Chorus

Verse two:
Hiking into some trees
Just me and them honey bees
With 75 pounds of gear on my back
Ya gonna see the country just like that
I know it's just like that
If it's rain snow or shine
So intimate it is to me
All of them woods and coastline
This wilderness is a part of me
This is my home away from home
Hiking into some wilderness
If I can't find my way back home
The sweat on my brow fallen down
The 75 pounds of gear on my back
Eagle please don't fail me now
Push just one more bend in that trek
With the sweat on my brow
I can see the Pacific Trail like that

....End song

By: Russell A. Clemo
Song Titled: **Kootenai Valley On That Yaak River**

Kootenai Valley On That Yaak River
You come to me in a dream
Out on that white water
I can dream anything
        Chorus

        Verse one:
Puttin my line in that water
Ya fish on the line
When my lure kisses that water
I'll be doing just fine
Drink me another beer honey
Ya fish on the line
Put some Neil Young on the radio
Let myself remember another time
Put my line in that water
It's more than a stream
I know every bend and creek
I know every little seam
When that river talks to me
I tell it everything
We talked about my first girlfriend
We talked about my first car
When I caught my first fish here honey
That's when I got my first scar

Kootenai Valley On That Yaak River
You come to me in a dream
Out on that white water
I can dream anything
        Chorus

Verse two:
Puttin my line in that water
Ya fish on the line
When my lure kisses that water
I'll be doing just fine
Drink me another beer honey
Ya fish on the line
Put some Neil Young on the radio
Let myself remember another time
Put my line in that water
It's more than a stream
I know every bend and creek
I know every little seam
When that river talks to me
I tell it everything
We talked about my first girlfriend
We talked about my first car
When I caught my first fish here honey
That's when I got my first scar

Kootenai Valley On That Yaak River
You come to me in a dream
Out on that white water
I can dream anything
        Chorus
                ....End song

Chapter:

A Great Book of American Songs (IV.)

Russell A. Clemo

INDEX

1. God's Tears Comen Down
2. The Rebel is Runnen
3. You Can Get It On The Run
4. Ain't Nothen Like These Stars
5. Singen Around The Campfire
6. It's The Taste From Your Lips
7. I Believe I Can Make You Happy
8. I Can Feel A Storm
9. I'm Not Waiting For You To Say Sorry
10. Tree Lines And Windmills

By: Russell A. Clemo
Song Titled: **God's Tears Comen Down**

God's Tears Comen Down
Comen down like rain
You can feel inside
I can see his pain
        Chorus

        Verse One:
I'm feeling stranded
Stranded here on earth
Every since I can feel
Every since my birth
Didn't think it then
I can feel inside
I know his pain
I can feel his pride
I know what is real honey
Ya everything that died
While he tries to let that go
I tried to let that go inside
I can see his pain
What doesn't wash away
Comen down like rain
Through thunder storms baby
I can see God's pain
What makes him all knowing
That's what keeps him sane
What plays in his mind
He keeps me sane
Drinkin from a whiskey bottle
Wash it all down with the whiskey
I know he remembers my name
He remembers my name

God's Tears Comen Down
Comen down like rain

You can feel inside
I can see his pain
  Chorus

  Verse Two:
I can see through time
While I'm standen here
I'm standen in a line
What was I waiten for
I could see the sign
I had to turn away
To turn back again
I had to give it all up
Now I'm taken it back again
Swimmen in some whiskey
Ya I'm swimmen in some sin
I can see God's pain
What doesn't wash away
Comen down like rain
Through thunder storms baby
I can see God's pain
What makes him all knowing
That's what keeps him sane
As it plays in his mind
That's what keeps me sane
Drinken from a whiskey bottle
You're drinken from that bottle
I wash it down with the whiskey
I know he remembers my name
He remembers my name

God's Tears Comen Down
Comen down like rain
You can feel inside
I can see his pain
  Chorus
    ….End song

By: Russell A. Clemo
Song Titled: **The Rebel is Runnen**

The Rebel is Runnen
His country jezebel is runnen
You can hear the sound
You can hear the sound
        Chorus

        Verse One:
There's desert sand darlen
Cactus on the ground
Canyon rock in the distance
While I'm looken around
Everything that I love
It's just outside of town
Find some cool water running
Ya it's on the ground
Ya I get my Johnson boat running
Just to hear the sound
Pull the Yeti cooler out
I'm gonna drink until I drown
This cowboy is running
It's on the ground running
She sees desert sand
She sees cactus all around
When she sees canyon rock
While she's looken around
Ya everything that I love
We're just outside of town
Me and my little darlen
Find some cool water running
It's on the ground
Ya it's on the ground

The Rebel is Runnen
His country jezebel is runnen

You can hear the sound
You can hear the sound
    Chorus

    Verse Two:
There's desert sand darlen
Cactus on the ground
Canyon rock in the distance
While I'm looken around
Everything that I love
It's just outside of town
Find some cool water running
Ya it's on the ground
Ya I get my Johnson boat running
Just to hear the sound
Pull the Yeti cooler out
I'm gonna drink until I drown
This cowboy is running
It's on the ground running
She sees desert sand
She sees cactus all around
When she sees canyon rock
While she's looken around
Ya everything that I love
We're just outside of town
Me and my little darlen
Find some cool water running
It's on the ground
Ya it's on the ground

The Rebel is Runnen
His country jezebel is runnen
You can hear the sound
You can hear the sound
    Chorus
        ....End song

By: Russell A. Clemo
Song Titled: **You Can Get It On The Run**

You Can Get It On The Run
I know what you want from me
It's plain for me to see
You can get it on the run
        Chorus

        Verse One:
I know you want to walk away
You walk away from me
I know what it means this time
Eyes so I can see
History and some time
What's between you and me
What will break us apart
You don't need to run away
Don't run away from me
If we stay here together
We can make this thing last
We can be sure to weather
Turn away from the past
We will turn to our future
Meet it with open arms
We can make it just like that
Just stay in my arms
Please stay in my arms

You Can Get It On The Run
I know what you want from me
It's plain for me to see
You can get it on the run
        Chorus

Verse Two:
I know you want to walk away
You walk away from me
I know what it means this time
Eyes so I can see
History and some time
What's between you and me
What will break us apart
You don't need to run away
Don't run away from me
If we stay here together
We can make this thing last
We can be sure to weather
Turn away from the past
We will turn to our future
Meet it with open arms
We can make it just like that
Just stay in my arms
Please stay in my arms

You Can Get It On The Run
I know what you want from me
It's plain for me to see
You can get it on the run
            Chorus
                    ….End song

By: Russell A. Clemo
Song Titled: **Ain't Nothen Like These Stars**

Ain't Nothen Like These Stars
Stars I see in your light
I can take you there little darlen
I seen Van Gogh paint a starry night
        Chorus

        Verse One:
A shooting star in the sky
Make a wish for me
Baby please don't tell me why
I'm looken to the heavens
I make a wish for you
A cowboy can dream forever
Baby what do we do
We're sitting out by a lake
It's just me and you
Ya we're sitting on a tailgate
We're looken at stars in the sky
Leaving us in wonder
It leaves a twinkle in my eye
You're my little sweetheart
What does it do for you
I'm looken in your eyes
I can see you twinkle too
Come on take my hand
A shooting star meant for two
Come on and take my hand
Ya it's meant for me and you
Little darlen don't you see
You're tail gaten right next to me
Ya you're sitten right next to me

Ain't Nothen Like These Stars
Stars I see in your light

I can take you there little darlen
I seen Van Gogh paint a starry night
        Chorus

        Verse Two:
A shooting star in the sky
Make a wish for me
Baby please don't tell me why
I'm looken to the heavens
I make a wish for you
A cowboy can dream forever
Ya it's twenty years later
We're sitting out by a lake
All my wishen it came true
Same truck same tail gate
It's still me and you
Another twist in the love
Another twist in our fate
Looken at stars in the sky
What is leaving us in wonder
It leaves a twinkle in my eye
You're my little sweetheart
I know what it does for you
I see you twinkle too
I'm looken in your eyes
A shooting star meant for two
Little darlen don't you see
You're tail gaten right next to me
Ya you're sitten right next to me

Ain't Nothen Like These Stars
Stars I see in your light
I can take you there little darlen
I seen Van Gogh paint a starry night
        Chorus
                ….End song

By: Russell A. Clemo
Song Titled: **Singen Around The Campfire**

Singen Around The Campfire
Another song about love
Ya a song about family
Those are the ones I'm thinken of
     Chorus

          Verse One:
A country campfire song
That's how we celebrate love
Singen campfire songs
The stars up above
Someone grab a guitar
The moon up above
Feel the love tonight
I feel the love tonight
Someone grab some drums
Let me hear them play
Let me hear your song
Feel the love this way
Someone grab a tambourine
Gather around the fire
A country campfire song
Let it take you higher
It's somewhere up above
I can feel the love

Singen Around The Campfire
Another song about love
Ya a song about family
Those are the ones I'm thinken of
     Chorus

Verse Two:
Help me sing a campfire song
Help me celebrate love
Singen campfire songs
The stars up above
Someone grab a guitar
The moon up above
Feel the love tonight
I feel the love tonight
You grab some drums
Let me hear them play
Let me hear your song
Feel the love this way
You grab a tambourine
Gather around the fire
A country campfire song
Let it take you higher
It's somewhere up above
I can feel the love

Singen Around The Campfire
Another song about love
Ya a song about family
Those are the ones I'm thinken of
Chorus
....End song

By: Russell A. Clemo
Song Titled: **It's The Taste From Your Lips**

It's The Taste From Your Lips
It's the taste from your kiss
I can feel you like this
I can feel you like this
        Chorus

        Verse One:
Dreams became the real
You're something I can feel
How you feel to me
Love and some tenderness
Love and some bliss
My heart meld inside of you
My body it melds inside of you
I do what you ask me to
I give you what you ask me to
Ya what becomes so painfully real
You tell me you have to feel
You tell me love and some tenderness
How you feel to me it's bliss
You tell me meld inside of you
You tell me honey baby
I do what you ask me to
Ya look inside me like this
Look inside me like this

It's The Taste From Your Lips
It's the taste from your kiss
I can feel you like this
I can feel you like this
        Chorus

Verse Two:
Dreams became the real
You're something I can feel
How you feel to me
Love and some tenderness
Love and some bliss
My heart meld inside of you
My body it melds inside of you
I do what you ask me to
I give you what you ask me to
Ya what becomes so painfully real
You tell me you have to feel
You tell me love and some tenderness
How you feel to me it's bliss
You tell me meld inside of you
You tell me honey baby
I do what you ask me to
Ya look inside me like this
Look inside me like this

It's The Taste From Your Lips
It's the taste from your kiss
I can feel you like this
I can feel you like this
Chorus
....End song

By: Russell A. Clemo
Song Titled: **I Believe I Can Make You Happy**

I Believe I Can Make You Happy
Trade dreams for broken things
I believe I can make you happy
Walken out on missing things
        Chorus

        Verse One:
What makes me happy
Dream for so many things
Girl you make me happy
Write it in the sand just for you
Darlen tell me what makes you happy
Ya girl that's what I'll do
I have dreams and ambition
I can spell it just for two
You read it just for me
Or you read it for me and you
This cowboy can be your daddy
I'm gonna tell you what we can do
Travel to each end of the earth
I show you what you are worth
One more trip around the world
I'm traden in on dreams
Honey no more broken things
We're walken out on broken things

I Believe I Can Make You Happy
Trade dreams for broken things
I believe I can make you happy
Walken out on missing things
        Chorus

Verse Two:
What makes you happy baby
You dream for so many things
Girl you make me happy
Write it in the sand for me and you
Tell me what makes you happy
Ya girl that's what I'll do
You have dreams and ambition
I can spell it just for two
You read it just for me
Or you read it for me and you
This cowboy can be your daddy
I'm gonna tell you what we can do
Travel to each end of the earth
I show you what you are worth
One more trip around the world
I'm traden in on dreams
Honey no more broken things
We're walken out on broken things

I Believe I Can Make You Happy
Trade dreams for broken things
I believe I can make you happy
Walken out on missing things
　　　Chorus
　　　　　....End song

 By: Russell A. Clemo
Song Titled: **I Can Feel A Storm**

I Can Feel A Storm
Rainy weather feel so warm
From distant shores I can see
Feeling distant I believe
      Chorus

      Verse One:
Feelings of being lost at sea
Ya something's in between
Memories I can see
They're giving pain to me
Remembering only in a dream
A life that's meant for me
One where we're happy
See the distant shores baby
Fade with my memories
We're getting older you and me
You helped me so I can see
Feeling distant I believe
Rainy weather feels so warm
You recognize this in me
Pull me in close baby
Eyes so I can see
That's why I love you baby
That's why you love me

I Can Feel A Storm
Rainy weather feel so warm
From distant shores I can see
Feeling distant I believe
      Chorus

Verse Two:
Feelings of being lost at sea
Ya something's in between
Memories I can see
They're giving pain to me
Remembering only in a dream
A life that's meant for me
One where we're happy
See the distant shores baby
Fade with my memories
We're getting older you and me
You helped me so I can see
Feeling distant I believe
Rainy weather feels so warm
You recognize this in me
Pull me in close baby
Eyes so I can see
That's why I love you baby
That's why you love me

....End song

By: Russell A. Clemo
Song Titled: **I'm Not Waiting For You To Say Sorry**

I'm Not Waiting For You To Say Sorry
I don't want any more stories
Let's make things different darlen
Still waiting for you to say sorry
  Chorus

  Verse One:
Every story line from me
Another reason from me
Only tell you what I won't do
Then I walk away from you
You want our history
I come back to you darlen
But we never say sorry
I'm maken love to you
What is maken up to you
How are you supposed to feel
Then I give you another story
Always steppen out on you
While you're so hot to me
You always take me back
Every time you're in a way
You know I need you just like that
Baby please make love to me
It's all about maken up to me

I'm Not Waiting For You To Say Sorry
I don't want any more stories
Let's make things different darlen
Still waiting for you to say sorry
  Chorus

Verse Two:
Every story line from you
Another reason from you
Only tell me what you won't do
Then you walk away from me
I want our history honey
You come back to me
But we never say sorry
You're maken love to me
What is maken up to me
How am I supposed to feel baby
Then you give me another story
Always steppen out on me
While you're so hot to me
I always take you back
Every time I'm in a way
I know you need me just like that
Baby please make love to me
It's all about maken up to me

I'm Not Waiting For You To Say Sorry
I don't want any more stories
Let's make things different darlen
Still waiting for you to say sorry
          Chorus
                  ….End song

By: Russell A. Clemo
Song Titled: **Tree Lines And Windmills**

Tree Lines And Windmills
When there's wind outside
No hills or mountains
Feel the wind outside
I left behind the Big Sky
For the North Dakota night
Just tree lines and windmills
Get me through the night
      Chorus

     Verse One:
Tree lines and windmills
Then I cozy up to you
We'll have wine then coffee
Maybe a candle or two
Just like the last time
Then I'll dance with you
Slow dance until morning
Then fall in bed with you
We'll make love in the morning
I'll cook breakfast for two
Ya I left behind the Big Sky
For the North Dakota night
I'm somewhere out on Highway 2
Thinken about my yesterdays
The days I spent with you
That's why I'm out here in the night
I wanna make love to you
Your love feels so right
The Arctic wind is blowen
It's blowen from the North tonight
But it won't stop me now
I gotta get back to you
I do whatever it takes
I gotta get back to you

Tree Lines And Windmills
When there's wind outside
No hills or mountains

Feel the wind outside
I left behind the Big Sky
For the North Dakota night
Just tree lines and windmills
Get me through the night
　　　Chorus

　　　Verse Two:
Tree lines and windmills
Then I cozy up to you
We'll have wine then coffee
Maybe a candle or two
Just like the last time
Then I'll dance with you
Slow dance until morning
Then fall in bed with you
We'll make love in the morning
I'll cook breakfast for two
Ya I left behind the Big Sky
For the North Dakota night
I'm somewhere out on Highway 2
Thinken about my yesterdays
The days I spent with you
That's why I'm out here in the night
I wanna make love to you
Your love feels so right
The Arctic wind is blowen
It's blowen from the North tonight
But it won't stop me now
I gotta get back to you
I do whatever it takes
I gotta get back to you

Tree Lines And Windmills
When there's wind outside
No hills or mountains
Feel the wind outside
I left behind the Big Sky
For the North Dakota night
Just tree lines and windmills
Get me through the night
　　　Chorus
　　　　　....End song

CHAPTER:

A Great Book of American Songs (V.)

Russell A. Clemo

INDEX

1. Walken A Crooked Dirt Road
2. When Heaven Comes Fallen Down
3. Can You Tell Me What's Left
4. She Said She Likes A Cowboy
5. Cowboy With A Six Gun
6. If You Love Americana
7. The Cowboy Will Never Die
8. There's An Early Morning Fog
9. When I Look In Your Eyes
10. Have You Ever Seen A North Dakota Light

By: Russell A. Clemo
Song Titled: **Walken A Crooked Dirt Road**

Walken A Crooked Dirt Road
Don't know how far I'll go
Don't wait for me baby
Don't wait to see which way I go
            Chorus

        Verse one:
A drifter on that line
All I need is a little love
Some love and some sunshine
My heart is yours baby
Your heart is mine
I've got a red Dixie cup
Drinken on some good wine
Don't wait for me baby
We can both have a good time
Do you need a little love
Do you need some sunshine
You can take my hand baby
I promise it feels so fine
Walken a crooked dirt road
We can share some good wine
You can walk with me baby
Together we're keepen time
Together it feels so fine

Walken a crooked dirt road
Don't know how far I'll go
Don't wait for me baby
Don't wait to see which way I go
            Chorus

Verse two:

She's a drifter on that line
All she needs is a little love
Some love and some sunshine
She says my heart is yours
Your heart is mine
I've got a red Dixie cup
Drinken on some good wine
Don't wait for me baby
We can both have a good time
She says do you need a little love
Do you need some sunshine
You can take my hand baby
Ya I promise it feels so fine
Walken a crooked dirt road
We can share some good wine
She says you can walk with me baby
Together we're keepen time
Together it feels so fine

Walken a crooked dirt road
Don't know how far I'll go
Don't wait for me baby
Don't wait to see which way I go
Chorus
....End song

By: Russell A. Clemo
Song Titled: **When Heaven Comes Fallen Down**

When heaven comes fallen down
Crashen into the ground
Ya something's comen over me
What it is to be free
   Chorus

   Verse one:
When the sky is falling
When it comes fallen down
Let it crash into the ground
You can hear the sound
Sing along with me
What it is to be free
The music's inside of me
You can feel it across the land
Come on and take my hand
When heaven comes fallen down
Nobodys left lookin around
Who's left looking around
What it is to be free
Brothers & sisters standen next to me
Each one has there own story
Each one singing set me free
Feel it all across the land
If the angel is in the music
Come on and take my hand
The music's inside of me
Not waiten on the angel and his mysteries
Ya baby we're gonna dance today
We're gonna make our way
Ya we're gonna make a way

When heaven comes fallen down
Crashen into the ground
Ya something's comen over me
What it is to be free
    Chorus

    Verse two:
When the sky is falling
When it comes fallen down
Let it crash into the ground
You can hear the sound
Sing along with me
What it is to be free
The music's inside of me
You can feel it across the land
Come on and take my hand
When heaven comes fallen down
Nobody's left looking around
Who's left looking around
What it is to be free
Brothers & sisters standen next to me
Each one has there own story
Each one singing set me free
Feel it all across the land
If the angel is in the music
Come on and take my hand
The music's inside of me
Not waiten on the angel and his mysteries
Ya baby we're gonna dance today
We're gonna make our way
Ya we're gonna make a way

When heaven comes fallen down
Crashen into the ground
Ya something's comen over me
What it is to be free
    Chorus
        ....End song

By: Russell A. Clemo
Song Titled: **Can You Tell Me What's Left**

Can you tell me what's left
What's left in your life
For what's wrong and what's right
Will you tell me what's left
      Chorus

      Verse one:
If you were wrong
If you were right
When its dark in your mind
When you start to lose sight
When the battle goes on
You will continue to fight
Will you fight for me
I need you here tonight
Rain is fallen down
I can see your light
Rain slipping through my hands
Won't wash away the night
What is killing you
It is the same thing
Same thing that gives you life
What is it gives you life
I need all of the pain
I need the love baby
I need you in that storm
I'm looken up above
It's rainen down on me
Rain slipping through my hands
Who do you want me to be
I'm gonna be that honest man

Can you tell me what's left
What's left in your life
For what's wrong and what's right
Will you tell me what's left
      Chorus

      Verse two:
If I was wrong
Ya if I was right
When it's dark in my mind
When I start to lose sight
When the battle goes on
I will continue to fight
Will you fight for me
I need you here tonight
Rain is fallen down
I can see your light
Rain slipping through my hands
Won't wash away the night
What is killing me
It is the same thing
Same thing that gives me life
What is it gives you life
I need all of the pain
I need the love baby
I need you in that storm
I'm looken up above
It's rainen down on me
Rain slipping through my hands
Who do you want me to be
I'm gonna be that honest man

Can you tell me what's left
What's left in your life
For what's wrong and what's right
Will you tell me what's left
      Chorus
        ....End song

By: Russell A. Clemo
Song Titled: **She Said She Likes A Cowboy**

She said she likes a cowboy
T-shirt and blue jeans on
She said she wants a cowboy
T-shirt and blue jeans on
    Chorus

    Verse one:
A can of Copenhagen
Wearen a hole in the pocket
And I'm wearen her heart
She wears mine in a locket
I got a T-shirt & blue jeans on
Ya darlin wants to come over to listen
Listen to her favorite cowboy songs
I got on a fresh Hanes baby
With some new Wranglers on
I know that drives you crazy
Ya we can dance all night long
Come on and kiss me baby
Radio play that song
Don't play with me baby
Dance with me all night long
We make it last forever
My T-shirt and blue jeans on
Make it last forever

She said she likes a cowboy
T-shirt and blue jeans on
She said she wants a cowboy
T-shirt and blue jeans on
    Chorus

Verse two:
A can of Copenhagen
Wearen a hole in the pocket
And I'm wearen her heart
She wears mine in a locket
I got a T-shirt & blue jeans on
Ya darlin wants to come over to listen
Listen to her favorite cowboy songs
I got on a fresh Hanes baby
With some new Wranglers on
I know that drives you crazy
Ya we can dance all night long
Come on and kiss me baby
Radio play that song
Don't play with me baby
Dance with me all night long
We make it last forever
My T-shirt and blue jeans on
Make it last forever

She said she likes a cowboy
T-shirt and blue jeans on
She said she wants a cowboy
T-shirt and blue jeans on
        Chorus
            ....End song

By: Russell A. Clemo
Song Titled: **Cowboy With A Six Gun**

Cowboy with a six gun
Cowboy stayen on the the run
Every outlaw out here under the sun
Ya they're looken at him
They know he is the one
        Chorus

        Verse one:
Take to the country
Stay on the lam
Stay runnen from a posse
I don't give a damn
I'll die from a shooter
Six gun in my hand
If I told you once boy
I'll die in this land
If you can't run with me
Then you ain't got sand
If you wanna call me brother
If you ride for a brand
Two in the bush
Worth one in the hand
Cowboy with a six gun
Six gun in my hand
If I told you once boy
I'll die in this land

Cowboy with a six gun
Cowboy stayen on the run
Every outlaw out here under the sun
Ya they're looken at him
They know he is the one
        Chorus

Verse two:
Every back dirt road
Every country mile
A cowboy stays runnen
I make it worth while
I like women and whiskey
Keep a low profile
I don't give a damn
If I told you once boy
I'll die in this land
If you can't run with me
Then you ain't got sand
If you don't ride with a six gun
If you ride for a brand
Two in the bush
Worth one in the hand
Cowboy with a six gun
If I told you once boy
I'll die in this land

Cowboy with a six gun
Cowboy stayen on the run
Every outlaw out here under the sun
Ya they're looken at him
They know he is the one
Chorus
....End song

By: Russell A. Clemo
Song Titled: **If You Love Americana**

If you love Americana
If you love honkey tonk
Let me see a cowgirl dance
Let me see a cowboy stomp
    Chorus

    Verse one:
Stomp if you want to see
See his spirit live on
Red blood and blue blood
You better sing along
Stomp if you wanna see
Line dance to this song
Let me see you front to back
You better sing along
Stomp if you wanna see
If you love Americana
If you love honkey tonk
Let me see a cowgirl dance
Let me see a cowboy stomp
Let me see you front to back
Let me hear it loud
Stomp if you wanna see
Line dance to this song
Sing along with me

If you love Americana
If you love honkey tonk
Let me see a cowgirl dance
Let me see a cowboy stomp
    Chorus

Verse two:
Stomp if you want to see
See his spirit live on
Red blood and blue blood
You better sing along
Stomp if you wanna see
Line dance to this song
Let me see you front to back
You better sing along
Stomp if you wanna see
If you love Americana
If you love honkey tonk
Let me see a cowgirl dance
Let me see a cowboy stomp
Let me see you front to back
Let me hear it loud
Stomp if you wanna see
Line dance to this song
Sing along with me

....End song

By: Russell A. Clemo
Song Titled: **The Cowboy Will Never Die**

The Cowboy Will Never Die
See the eagle fly
I don't need to wonder why
The cowboy will never die
        Chorus

        Verse one:
Who is that boy
Watch his spirit fly
Let his spirit live on
Don't watch as it dies
Give some truth to the eagle
I don't need to wonder why
The patriot is something renewed
The cowboy will never die
When I'm looken to the heavens
When I'm looken to the sky
If I'm throwing up a Prayer
Go on and watch my spirit fly
If you throw up a Prayer
Then we can get high
Let the cowboy live forever
Hear the cowboy cry
If he's looken at you
He looked an eagle in his eye

The cowboy will never die
See the eagle fly
I don't need to wonder why
The cowboy will never die
        Chorus

Verse two:
Who is that boy
Watch his spirit fly
Let his spirit live on
Don't watch as it dies
Give some truth to the eagle
I don't need to wonder why
The patriot is something renewed
The cowboy will never die
When I'm looken to the heavens
When I'm looken to the sky
If I'm throwing up a Prayer
Go on and watch my spirit fly
If you throw up a Prayer
Then we can get high
Let the cowboy live forever
Hear the cowboy cry
If he's looken at you
He looked an eagle in his eye

....End song

By: Russell A. Clemo
Song Titled: **There's An Early Morning Fog**

There's an early morning fog
Smoke on that water
Just me and my dog
Put my boat in that water
    Chorus

        Verse one:
Drift wood on that water
Rollen down that stream
Floating on that water
Come to me in a dream
Sun shrank that water
Turn the water into a stream
Bring me some rain
Wake me from my dream
Water refills that river
It replenishes everything
I live on that water
It means everything
Put my boat in that water
Love to hear the motor sing
Fish on that line
As I watch that water sing
I can see that sign
Fish on that line

There's an early morning fog
Smoke on that water
Just me and my dog
Put my boat in that water
    Chorus

Verse two:
Drift wood on that water
Rollen down that stream
Floating on that water
Come to me in a dream
Sun shrank that water
Turn the water into a stream
Bring me some rain
Wake me from my dream
Water refills that river
It replenishes everything
I live on that water
It means everything
Put my boat in that water
Love to hear the motor sing
Fish on that line
As I watch that water sing
I can see that sign
Fish on that line

....End song

By: Russell A. Clemo
Song Titled: **When I Look In Your Eyes**

When I look in your eyes
I can't bring myself to say goodbyes
When I look at you
There's nothing that I wouldn't do
        Chorus

        Verse one:
If we have to part
If we have to part for awhile
Let's stay in and make love
Let's say goodbye for awhile
Darlin there's nothen I wouldn't do
I'll pull out some candles
I'll prepare dinner for two
We'll talk about the future
When I'll reunite with you
When I look in your eyes
I only wanna be with you
I don't wanna say goodbyes
When we are apart
That's when I'm missen you
Let's stay in and make love
Darlin we still have tonight
I'll try to make it last forever
We'll make it last forever

When I look in your eyes
I can't bring myself to say goodbyes
When I look at you
There's nothing I wouldn't do
        Chorus

Verse two:
When I look at you
My heart gives a start
I hope you can stay awhile
Let's stay in and make love
Let's stay here for awhile
Darlin there's nothen I wouldn't do
I'll put on some good music
I'll slow dance with you
We'll talk about the future
When I look in your eyes
I only wanna be with you
I don't wanna say goodbyes
When we are apart
That's when I'm missen you
Let's stay in and make love
Darlin we still have tonight
I'll try to make it last forever
We'll make it last forever

....End song

By: Russell A. Clemo
Song Titled: **Have You Ever Seen A North Dakota Light**

Have You Ever Seen A North Dakota Light
Have you ever seen it in the dusk
Living deep in the heartland
Living in the heartland with us
     Chorus

     Verse One
The wind is blowing in
Blowing in from across a lake
I can see from my porch
I can see across a wake
Looking at a distant horizon
It's a beautiful horizon
As the water glistens on Stump Lake
What brings us together
Ya as we look out on that lake
Have you ever seen a North Dakota light
Have you ever seen it in the dusk
Living deep in the heartland
Living in the heartland with us
What we share in this life
Give it with love and trust
Let the wind keep blowing in
Ya keep blowing in with the dusk
Have you ever seen a North Dakota light

Have You Ever Seen A North Dakota Light
Have you ever seen it in the dusk
Living deep in the heartland
Living in the heartland with us
     Chorus

Verse Two
Sunshine splays across a lake
Sunshine splayed in the dusk
I can see from my porch
I can see across a wake
Looking at a distant horizon
It's a beautiful horizon
As the water glistens on Stump Lake
What brings us together
Ya as we look out on that lake
Have you ever seen a North Dakota light
Have you ever seen it in the dusk
Living deep in the heartland
Living in the heartland with us
What we share in this life
Give it with love and trust
Let sunshine splay across that lake
Ya sunshine splay in that dusk
Have you ever seen a North Dakota light

Have You Ever Seen A North Dakota Light
Have you ever seen it in the dusk
Living deep in the heartland
Living in the heartland with us
Chorus
....End song

CHAPTER:

A Great Book of American Songs (VI.)

Russell A. Clemo

INDEX

1. I Gave Her A Garden
2. Feels Like I'm Standen Still
3. Over The Years Darlin
4. Kid Rock And Cheryl Crow
5. Look Into My Eyes Baby
6. His Heart Is Not With You
7. I Know Your Favorite Is Tequila
8. It's The Light In Your Eyes
9. Tender With A Subtle Smokiness
10. The Greatest Gifts Baby

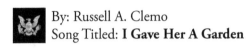 By: Russell A. Clemo
Song Titled: **I Gave Her A Garden**

I Gave Her A Garden
That's where everything grows
She knows if she needs me
That this cowboy goes
        Chorus

        Verse one:
A cowboy and a Rose
I can see her now
She is looken at me
She's asken me how
How do we make it
How do we make it last
Turn to our future
Turn way from our past
She says she wants a cowboy
A cowboy and a rose
I told her I'll be that man
We'll see how far this goes
We can make it last
Turn to our future
Turn away from the past
We can do this forever
Ya a cowboy and a rose
A cowboy and a rose

I Gave Her A Garden
That's where everything grows
She knows if she need me
That this cowboy goes
        Chorus

Verse two:
A cowboy and a rose
I can see her now
She is looken at me
She's asken me how
I told her diamonds
Diamonds are forever
Let's turn to our future
Turn away from the past
She says she wants a cowboy
A cowboy and a rose
I gave her a garden
That's where everything grows
She knows if she needs me
That this cowboy goes
I'll work harder for her
I'll give her everything
Ya a cowboy and a rose
A cowboy and a rose

I Gave Her A Garden
That's where everything grows
She knows if she need me
That this cowboy goes
Chorus
....End song

By: Russell A. Clemo
Song Titled: **Feels Like I'm Standen Still**

Feels Like I'm Standen Still
Standen still in time
She's her father's daughter
She looks so fine
        Chorus

        Verse one:
I knew she was a friend
She's a friend of mine
It was in her smile
I'm looken at it
Looken at it all the time
The sparkle in her eyes
Feels like I'm standen still
Standen still in time
She's her father's daughter
She looks so fine
I think I'll ask him
I'd like to make her mine
Ask for his blessing
I'd ask a million times
As the seasons change
She feels so fine
My feelings don't change
Feels like I'm standen still

Feels like I'm standen still
Standen still in time
She's her father's daughter
She looks so fine
        Chorus

Verse two:
I knew she was a friend
She's a friend of mine
Now that we're getting married
No time to rewind
Time for maken babies
Shes already made up her mind
Feels like I'm standen still
Standen still in time
She's her father's daughter
She looks so fine
Give him some grandchildren
Now that I made her mine
Glad I got his blessing
I had to ask a million times
As the seasons change
My feelings don't change
Ya she feels so fine
Feels like I'm standen still

....End song

By: Russell A. Clemo
Song Titled: **Over The Years Darlin**

Over the years darlin
Throughout the years ahead
What will be will be
Together as we look ahead
    Chorus

    Verse one:
A different space
Our space and time
A different heart
Your heart is mine
Light before your shadow
I can see in time
I watch the light in your eyes
Thank the stars that your mine
I'm looken to the heavens
You sent me a sign
Something's smiling down on me
Ya I thank the stars that your mine
You and me over the years darlin
We can make a love like this
It's you and me baby
All I need is your kiss
Take my hand baby
We can make a life like this

Over the years darlin
Throughout the years ahead
What will be will be
Together as we look ahead
    Chorus

Verse two:
A different space
Our space and time
A different heart
Your heart is mine
Light before your shadow
I can see in time
I watch the light in your eyes
Thank the stars that you're mine
I'm looken to the heavens
You sent me a sign
Something's smiling down on me
Ya I thank the stars that your mine
You and me over the years darlin
We can make a love like this
It's you and me baby
All I need is your kiss
Take my hand baby
We can make a life like this

Over the years darlin
Throughout the years ahead
What will be will be
Together as we look ahead
Chorus
....End song

By: Russell A. Clemo
Song Titled: **Kid Rock And Cheryl Crow**

Kid Rock and Cheryl Crow
They're playen on the radio
I'm looken at you Darlin
Tell me which way to go
            Chorus

        Verse one:
I'm looken at you Darlin
Tell me which way to go
Kid Rock and Cheryl Crow
They're playen on the radio
We're both looken out the window
Looken out of that pickup truck
I know we're fallen on hard times
All we need is a little luck
Baby as long as we're together
You and me and this pickup truck
I'm looken at you darlin
Tell me which way to go
Kid Rock and Cheryl Crow
They're playen on the radio
We'll find it in the next town
Keep a lookout honey darlin
The next will be comen around
Ya our luck will be comen around
We'll find it in a new town
We'll tie it all down
We'll get a nice little house
Now how does that sound
I'll get you a nice little house baby
Ya we'll tie it all down

Kid Rock and Cheryl Crow
They're playen on the radio

I'm looken at you Darlin
Tell me which way to go
          Chorus

          Verse two:
I'm looken at you Darlin
Tell me which way to go
Kid Rock and Cheryl Crow
They're playen on the radio
We're both looken out the window
Looken out of that pickup truck
I know we're fallen on hard times
All we need is a little luck
Baby as long as we're together
You and me and this pickup truck
I'm looken at you darlin
Tell me which way to go
Kid Rock and Cheryl Crow
They're playen on the radio
We'll find it in the next town
Keep a lookout honey darlin
The next will be comen around
Ya our luck will be comen around
We'll find it in a new town
We'll tie it all down
We'll get a nice little house
Now how does that sound
I'll get you a nice little house baby
Ya we'll tie it all down

Kid Rock and Cheryl Crow
They're playen on the radio
I'm looken at you Darlin
Tell me which way to go
          Chorus
               ….End song

By: Russell A. Clemo
Song Titled: **Look Into My Eyes Baby**

Look into my eyes baby
Don't need to look anywhere else
Just look into my eyes baby
That's where everything is felt
    Chorus

    Verse one:
When you look at me baby
Everything that is heart felt
You know it drives me crazy
That's why I call you my baby
I need you right here
Want you to look into my eyes
Ya want you to dance with me
Holding you close all through the night
I love to treat you like a lady
Let you know everything will be alright
Won't you dance with me baby
We'll dance all through the night
I'll build up a big fire
I'll create some candle light
We'll turn down the bed covers
We'll fall in bed late tonight
I wanna feel your lips baby
You make everything feel alright

Look into my eyes baby
Don't need to look anywhere else
Just look into my eyes baby
That's where everything is felt
    Chorus

Verse two:
When I look at you baby
Don't close your eyes when you kiss me
When your looken back at me
Ya I want you to see
Don't miss a moment with me baby
I need you here next to me
We'll create our forever
We'll create some ecstacy
Won't you dance with me baby
Holding you close all through the night
We'll sip white wine & champagne
I got your favorite candles that you like
I built us a great big fire
You can see it's burnen so bright
Rose petals in the bed covers
When we fall in bed late tonight
I wanna feel your lips kiss me baby
Darlin you make everything feel alright

Look into my eyes baby
Don't need to look anywhere else
Just look into my eyes baby
That's where everything is felt
        Chorus
                ....End song

By: Russell A. Clemo
Song Titled: **His Heart Is Not With You**

His heart is not with you
While you are here with me
I'm who you want me to be
I'll be here waiting patiently
        Chorus

        Verse one:
I am thinking of you
I'm waiting patiently
I am wanting you
I want to set you free
I come to you as a friend
Hopen that you will see
You know what we share honey
You could see a different side of me
While you're with him baby
While you are with me
His heart is not with you honey
I'm who you want me to be
He's always running around
I know that you can see
I've been waiting here honey
Telling you how you could be free
Why are you still there with him
You could be here next to me

His heart is not with you
While you are here with me
I'm who you want me to be
I'll be here waiting patiently
        Chorus

Verse two:
I am thinking of you
I'm waiting patiently
I am wanting you
I want to set you free
I come to you as a friend
Hopen that you will see
You know what we share honey
You could see a different side of me
While you're with him baby
While you are with me
His heart is not with you honey
I'm who you want me to be
He's always running around
I know that you can see
I've been waiting here honey
Telling you how you could be free
Why are you still there with him
You could be here next to me

His heart is not with you
While you are here with me
I'm who you want me to be
I'll be here waiting patiently
            Chorus
                    ....End song

By: Russell A. Clemo
Song Titled: **I Know Your Favorite Is Tequila**

I know your favorite is tequila
Fix you consuela or Margarita
Your favorite saying darlin
Hey it's nice to meet ya
    Chorus

    Verse one:
Everyday spent on the beach
Toes in the sand
Bar is on the beach
Friends in the sand
Come on and bring your baby
Bring it darlin and take my hand
You and me we'll retire this way
This is how we'll spend our days
Everybody singen the same tune
Hey its nice to meet ya
Your favorite is my favorite
Fix you consuela or Margarita
We meet our friends on the beach
We put our toes in the sand
We make this our forever
On a little piece of God's land
Create us some new moments
Hey its nice to meet ya

I know your favorite is tequila
Fix you consuela or Margarita
Your favorite saying darlin
Hey it's nice to meet ya
    Chorus

Verse two:
Everyday spent on the beach
Toes in the sand
Bar is on the beach
Friends in the sand
That's how I met you baby
I asked you to take my hand
You and me we'll retire this way
This is how we'll spend our days
Now I'm singen her tune
Hey it's nice to meet ya
Her favorite is my favorite
Fix her consuela or Margarita
We meet our friends on the beach
We put our toes in the sand
We make this our forever
On a little piece of God's land
Create us some new moments
Hey its nice to meet ya

....End song

By: Russell A. Clemo
Song Titled: **It's The Light In Your Eyes**

It's the light in your eyes
Your imagination that you share
Every thought intimate to me honey
I know you can feel me everywhere
    Chorus

    Verse one:
It's the light in your eyes
It's your cute little nose ring
My heart beats for you
Ya it's every little thing
It's your Monroe diamond stud
It's the ringlet curls in your hair
It's everything about you baby
I can feel you everywhere
It's the light in your eyes
Your imagination that you share
Every thought intimate to me honey
I know you can feel me everywhere
With your sexy cable knit sweaters
Ya I love your jeans with high heels
Caress your cheek tell you I care
I promise to show you how much I care
Tuck a hair tendril behind your ear
Remember and I'll be right there

It's the light in your eyes
Your imagination that you share
Every thought intimate to me honey
I know you can feel me everywhere
    Chorus

Verse two:
It's the light in your eyes
It's your shy look honey
My heart beats for you
When you look up at me
I know that it's true
I love to kiss your lips
I want to entangle with you
It's everything about your kiss
I can feel you everywhere its true
It's the light in your eyes
It's the color of your hair
It's your imagination inside your mind
Your imagination that you share
You know when I'm not with you honey
I know you can feel me everywhere
That's when I'm missing you baby
I promise to show you how much I care
Remember and I'll be right there

....End song

By: Russell A. Clemo
Song Titled: **Tender With A Subtle Smokiness**

Tender with a subtle smokiness
That's the kiss you get from my lips
That's a love with some tenderness
Ya it's a love with some tenderness
     Chorus

     Verse one:
Tender with a subtle smokiness
When it's you and me baby
There is a love like this
Ya slow dancing and tenderness
When you look at me honey
You say there's a subtle smokiness
That's the kiss you get from my lips
Come on darlin slow dance with me
You and me your my everything
Ya for you my heart will sing
I'm naked on the edge of the bed
I'm gonna play my guitar for you
After a long slow dance with you
There isn't anything that I wouldn't do
Slow dance and fall into bed
Ya let me do for you
We'll be maken love all through the night
I said baby let me do for you

Tender with a subtle smokiness
That's the kiss you get from my lips
That's a love with some tenderness
Ya it's a love with some tenderness
     Chorus

Verse two:
Tender with a subtle smokiness
When it's you and me baby
There is a love like this
Ya slow dancing and tenderness
When you look at me honey
You say there's a subtle smokiness
That's the kiss you get from my lips
Come on darlin slow dance with me
You and me your my everything
Ya for you my heart will sing
I'm naked on the edge of the bed
I'm gonna play my guitar for you
After a long slow dance with you
There isn't anything that I wouldn't do
Slow dance and fall into bed
Ya let me do for you
We'll be maken love all through the night
I said baby let me do for you

Tender with a subtle smokiness
That's the kiss you get from my lips
That's a love with some tenderness
Ya it's a love with some tenderness
Chorus
....End song

By: Russell A. Clemo
Song Titled: **The Greatest Gifts Baby**

The Greatest Gifts Baby
Greatest Gifts you can ever own
It's not found in gift shops baby
It's found inside of your home
     Chorus

     Verse one:
I'll give you those gifts baby
I'll give you a happy home
We can raise some children
Love them until they're grown
Ya we can foster a love
Ya until each their own
I'll be your man honey baby
Ya this will be our happy home
I'll give you the greatest gifts baby
It's found inside of your home
Ain't no ifs ands or maybes
Ya so find your way back home
Seeing that look in your eyes baby
It's felt in the heart of your home
In the heart of your loving family
Feel them calling you back home
Ya until we dearly depart
until we dearly depart

The Greatest Gifts Baby
Greatest Gifts you can ever own
It's not found in gift shops baby
It's found inside of your home
     Chorus

Verse two:
Let me give you those gifts baby
You make this a happy home
We can raise our children
Love them until they're grown
You create that love baby
Until each of them are grown
I'll be your man honey baby
Ya this'll be our happy home
You give me the greatest gifts
They're found inside of your home
Ain't no ifs ands or maybes
So baby find your way back home
Seeing that look in your eyes
It's felt in the heart of your home
In the heart of your loving family
Feel them calling you back home
Ya until we dearly depart
Until we dearly depart

The Greatest Gifts Baby
Greatest Gifts you can ever own
It's not found in gift shops baby
It's found inside of your home
Chorus
....End song

CHAPTER:

A Great Book of American Songs (VII.)

Russell A. Clemo

INDEX

1. Smoke With Me Baby
2. It's Not How You Fall Down
3. Don't Fade Away Honey
4. I Know Stars Can Align
5. The Dice Are Loaded
6. Blood Sweat And Tears
7. I'm Your Beautiful Magic
8. She Keeps Stealing Thunder
9. Love Peace And Contentment
10. There's A Special Place In Paradise

By: Russell A. Clemo
Song Titled: **Smoke With Me Baby**

Smoke With Me Baby
I ain't gotta choke
You gotta roll with me baby
You know I got that smoke
         Chorus

         Verse one:
Summer time on some water
Riden in that boat
Land it in that water
Let the good times float
If your my summer time baby
Electric guitar playen a perfect note
Cut off jeans and bikini ladies
Now who has got that smoke
Smoke with me baby
I ain't got to choke
You gotta roll with me baby
You know I got that smoke
Boats cutten through the water
You know we're riden now
Let the sun make it hotter
Got the girls screamen loud
You know your boys really got her
Brothers riden with me now

Smoke With Me Baby
I ain't gotta choke
You gotta roll with me baby
You know I got that smoke
         Chorus

Verse two:
Summer time on that water
Who riden in that boat
Land it in that water
Everybody let the good times float
If your that summer time baby
Ya guitars play a perfect note
Board shorts and bikini ladies
Now who's got that smoke
Smoke with me baby
I ain't got to choke
You gotta roll with me baby
You know I got that smoke
Now baby cutten through the water
You know we're riden now
Let the sun make it hotter
Got the girls screamen loud
You know your boys really got her
Brothers riden with me now

Smoke With Me Baby
I ain't gotta choke
You gotta roll with me baby
You know I got that smoke
            Chorus
                    ....End song

By: Russell A. Clemo
Song Titled: **It's Not How You Fall Down**

It's Not How You Fall Down
It's how you get back up
When you're fallen on hard times
When you're down on your luck
    Chorus

    Verse One:
It's not how you fall down
It's how you get back up
If you're tryen honey
You feelen like you're stuck
I'm tellen you darlin
You and that old pickup truck
I know you're fallen on hard times
Ya it's how you get back up
I can see you tryen honey
Tryen to make an honest buck
I'm tryen to be there for you darlin
Ya I hope that its enough
I'm the wind beneath your wings
Ya you need to get back up
Now I'm tellen you darlin
You and that old pickup truck
Ya I'm tellen you honey
You an that old pickup truck

It's Not How You Fall Down
It's how you get back up
When you're fallen on hard times
When you're down on your luck
    Chorus

Verse Two:
It's not how you fall down
It's how you get back up
If you're tryen honey
You feelen like you're stuck
I'm tellen you darlin
You and that old pickup truck
I know you're fallen on hard times
Ya it's how you get back up
I can see you tryen honey
Tryen to make an honest buck
I'm tryen to be there for you darlin
Ya I hope that its enough
I'm the wind beneath your wings
Ya you need to get back up
Now I'm tellen you darlin
You and that old pickup truck
Ya I'm tellen you honey
You an that old pickup truck

It's Not How You Fall Down
It's how you get back up
When you're fallen on hard times
When you're down on your luck
Chorus
....End song

By: Russell A. Clemo
Song Titled: **Don't Fade Away Honey**

Don't fade away honey
Fly for me now
What moves you baby
Move for me now
    Chorus

    Verse one:
Let your spirit take you
Let it fill your heart
Let it take you honey
From the very start
Levels of emotion
Your mind in part
What moves you baby
Let it fill your heart
It's washen over you
It's there to stay
Let it be in the night
Then comes a brand new day
Let me take you baby
I'll give you wings
When you're here on earth
It's the finer things
What moves you baby
It's washen over you

Don't Fade Away Honey
Fly for me now
What moves you baby
Move for me now
    Chorus

Verse two:
When your spirit takes you
When the stars align
Let it take you honey
That's when you're mine
I can hold you here
Your heart and mind
If your spirit's searchen for me
I ain't hard to find
What moves you baby
Let it fill your heart
To what ends honey
I was there from the start
Let me take you baby
I'll give you wings
When you're here on earth
It's the finer things
What moves you baby
It's washen over you

Don't Fade Away Honey
Fly for me now
What moves you baby
Move for me now
Chorus
....End song

By: Russell A. Clemo
Song Titled: **I Know Stars Can Align**

I know stars can align
What of embryonic stars you can't see
My emotions are bled for you
How can my spirit be free
      Chorus

      Verse one:
There's a different light
A different light in your stars
As I look up at you
Feeling all of my scars
Where is the cut I can't see
What is will be honey
But what about you and me
I know stars can align
What of embryonic stars you can't see
My emotions are bled for you
How can my spirit be free
What about the cuts
The cuts only you can see
What is on the other side honey
That's when we both will set free
What is on the ground
What is inside of me
There is a different light

I Know Stars Can Align
What of embryonic stars you can't see
My emotions are bled for you
How can my spirit be free
      Chorus

Verse two:
There is a different light
Where a star is born
Embryonic stars honey
That is where they are shorn
Those nebula in the skies
When I am looking at you
It's through these wandering eyes
I'm tryen to find you
Help me find my home
If I am wandering
Don't let me do it alone
Gasses of brilliant color
As I move through each night
A different space and time
My star is so bright
I can feel you inside
Please help me fight
There is a different light

I Know Stars Can Align
What of embryonic stars you can't see
My emotions are bled for you
How can my spirit be free
    Chorus
        ....End song

By: Russell A. Clemo
Song Titled: **The Dice Are Loaded**

The dice are loaded
So is the gun
I'm a gamblen man
Outlaw on the run
        Chorus

        Verse one:
I'm a gangster
Ride a motorcycle till I die
A fresh pair of sunglasses on
I looked the devil in his eye
There's a bandana around my face
But you can hear me cry
I can hear the wolf
I ain't gotta try
The dice are loaded
So is the gun
I'm a gamblen man
Outlaw on the run
I ride the circuits
I chase the sun
When it's dark as night
I am the one
I'm a gamblen man
Outlaw on the run

The Dice Are Loaded
So is the gun
I'm a gamblen man
Outlaw on the run
        Chorus

Verse two:
I'm a cowboy
Ride a motorcycle till I die
A fresh pair of leathers on
I looked the devil in his eye
There's a bandana on my face
But you can hear me cry
Ya you can hear the wolf
Honey you ain't gotta try
The dice are loaded
So is the gun
I'm a gamblen man
Outlaw on the run
You ride the circuits
You chase the sun
When it's dark as night
I am the one
I'm a gamblen man
Outlaw on the run

The Dice Are Loaded
So is the gun
I'm a gamblen man
Outlaw on the run
Chorus
....End song

By: Russell A. Clemo
Song Titled: **Blood Sweat And Tears**

Blood sweat and tears
Worken for the sweat
Blood sweat and tears
I'm worken for the sweat
        Chorus

        Verse one:
I wanna see music
See the music sweat
I wanna see blood and sweat
I wanna see tears
Baby we ain't done yet
Won't you dance for me honey
Someone play the next fret
What's playen on me
Baby we ain't done yet
Blood sweat and tears
Worken for the sweat
You wanna see music
See the music sweat
Your dancen for me honey
Let me see you sweat
I'm telling you let go
Someone play the next fret
Baby ain't no need to fret

Blood sweat and tears
Worken for the sweat
Blood sweat and tears
I'm worken for the sweat
        Chorus

Verse two:
I wanna see music
See the music sweat
I wanna see blood and sweat
I wanna see tears
Baby we ain't done yet
Won't you dance for me honey
Someone play the next fret
What's playen on me
Baby we ain't done yet
Blood sweat and tears
Worken for the sweat
You wanna see music
See the music sweat
Your dancen for me honey
Let me see you sweat
I'm telling you let go
Someone play the next fret
Baby ain't no need to fret

Blood sweat and tears
Worken for the sweat
Blood sweat and tears
I'm worken for the sweat
Chorus
....End song

By: Russell A. Clemo
Song Titled: **I'm Your Beautiful Magic**

I'm Your Beautiful Magic
I'm your white horse
Let me see your grace
I am a light source
I'm your white magic
I can feel your force
  Chorus

  Verse one:
What's inside of that
An animal is born
What lives inside
A heart is torn
Let me tell you honey
My heart is worn
White horse magic
Beautiful in a grace
Baby dance for me
It's inside your face
Won't you dance for me
We're wild and free
Don't cage the animal
Honey set me free
Two hearts are runnen
Ya you're with me
Let's make magic baby
So their eyes can see

I'm Your Beautiful Magic
I'm your white horse
Let me see your grace
I am a light source
I'm your white magic
I can feel your force
  Chorus

A Great Book of American Songs

Verse two:
What's inside of you
Your animal is born
What lives inside
When a heart is torn
Let me tell you honey
If your heart is worn
White horse magic
Beautiful in a grace
Honey dance for me
It's inside of your face
I know you'll dance for me
We're wild and free
Don't cage the animal baby
Come on and set it free
Two hearts are runnen
Ya you're runnen with me
Let's make magic baby
So their eyes can see

I'm Your Beautiful Magic
I'm your white horse
Let me see your grace
I am a light source
I'm your white magic
I can feel your force
Chorus
....End song

By: Russell A. Clemo
Song Titled: **She Keeps Stealing Thunder**

She keeps stealing thunder
She wants it from me
Ya it makes me wonder baby
Is she really that into me
        Chorus

        Verse one:
When I'm maken bad decisions
When I'm on the run
With whiskey in my veins
She tells me you are the one
All night runnen honey
I need to have some fun
I'll come back to you in the mornen
When comes the mornen sun
No time for dreams baby
No time for your light
Only time for runnen honey
Ya do it every night
Tonight you can ride with me baby
You can see what it's like
A jeep with the top down honey
Maybe we'll take my motorbike
As long as we're runnen honey
She keeps stealing thunder

She Keeps Stealing Thunder
She wants it from me
Ya it makes me wonder baby
Is she really that into me
        Chorus

Verse two:
When she's maken bad decisions
When I'm on the run
The whiskey in her veins
She tells me you are the one
All night runnen honey
She needs to have some fun
I'll come back to you in the mornen
When comes the mornen sun
No time for dreams baby
No time for your light
Only time for runnen honey
Ya do it every night
Tonight you can ride with me baby
You can see what it's like
A jeep with the top down honey
Maybe we'll take my motorbike
As long as we're runnen honey
She keeps stealing thunder

She Keeps Stealing Thunder
She wants it from me
Ya it makes me wonder baby
Is she really that into me
Chorus
....End song

By: Russell A. Clemo
Song Titled: **Love Peace And Contentment**

Love peace and contentment
That's what I need
Love peace and contentment
Ya that's what I need from you
     Chorus

     Verse one:
Love and some peace
When I find my stars
What I want from you
After some early scars
Ya peace and contentment
We're all following some shooting stars
See one touch the ground
Now here we are
Love peace and contentment
She falls to the ground
A star takes my hand
You place my heart
Now it's in your hands
If it isn't in your eyes
You said it's in my plans
Baby I will be for you
If that's what you need
That's what I need too

Love Peace And Contentment
That's what I need
Love peace and contentment
Ya that's what I need from you
     Chorus

Verse two:
Love and some peace
Looken at some stars
What I want from you
After some early scars
Ya peace and contentment
We're all following some shooting stars
See one touch the ground
Now here we are
Love peace and contentment
One falls to the ground
A star takes my hand
You place your heart
Now it's in my hands
If it isn't in my eyes
You said it's in your plans
Baby I will be for you
If that's what you need
That's what I need too

Love Peace And Contentment
That's what I need
Love peace and contentment
Ya that's what I need from you
Chorus
....End song

By: Russell A. Clemo
Song Titled: **There's A Special Place In Paradise**

There's a special place in Paradise
There's a place for you and me
Believe and baby you will see
There's a special place in Paradise
    Chorus

    Verse one:
A place we can hold hands
We can be together honey
A place for us to romance
We can dance together
I'll wait for you there
If you'll wait for me
A place for us to be free
We can't go there now
Its a place for tomorrow
There's a special place in Paradise
There's a place for you and me
Believe baby and you will see
Watch until the end of time
Then a new vision will become
I'll be waiting there for you
Baby it will be done
I can be there for you
There's a special place in Paradise

There's a special place in Paradise
There's a place for you and me
Believe and baby you will see
There's a special place in Paradise
    Chorus

Verse two:
Clouds we can hold in our hands
We can be together honey
A place of inifinite rainbows
We can dance together
I'll wait for you there
If you'll wait for me
A place for us to be free
We can't go there now
It's a place for tomorrow
There's a special place in Paradise
There's a place for you and me
Believe baby and you will see
Watch until the end of time
Then a new vision will become
I'll be waiting there for you
Baby it will be done
I can be there for you
There's a special place in Paradise

There's a special place in Paradise
There's a place for you and me
Believe and baby you will see
There's a special place in Paradise
Chorus
....End song

Chapter:

A Great Book of American Songs (VIII.)

Russell A. Clemo

INDEX

1. Forever You Stand By Me
2. It Was Written On The Winds
3. The Way Your Lips Taste
4. If I Knew Not
5. She's Talken To You True
6. I'm Lost And I Can't Be Found
7. She Won't Let Me Down
8. My Heart Has Gone To Ground
9. Hang On To Your Every Word
10. Love You More Than Anything

By: Russell A. Clemo
Song Titled: **Forever You Stand By Me**

Forever you stand by me
You are mine faithfully
Ya what it is to be
What it is when you're with me
        Chorus

        Verse one:
The winds of change
Baby at our backs
When we're runnen
You're runnen with me
That's when I'm liven facts
We're wild and free
Unplug all the jacks
We won't answer calls
We'll be out in the night
Knock down all the walls
Looking at you in the night
A star that never falls
Baby taste my lips
I taste your lips
Walk around the city
We're hand in hand
Place your heart in mine
Honey forever we stand

Forever you stand by me
You are mine faithfully
Ya what it is to be
What it is when you're with me
        Chorus

Verse two:
The moonlit sky
Baby at our backs
When we're liven
You're liven with me
That's when you're runnen facts
We're wild and free
Unplug all the jacks
Please don't answer calls
We'll be out all night
Knock down all the walls
Looking at me in the night
A star never falls
You taste my lips
I taste your lips
Runnen around the city
We're hand in hand
Place your heart in mine
Honey forever we stand

Forever you stand by me
You are mine faithfully
Ya what it is to be
What it is when you're with me
Chorus
....End song

By: Russell A. Clemo
Song Titled: **It Was Written On The Winds**

It was written on the winds
How will it perpetuate baby
Tell me who wins
If we win together
      Chorus

      Verse one:
I can hold clever conversations
When you're not talking to me
I can muse in a spell
Please talk to me
A clever girl in my head
Won't you be with me
Won't you sleep in my bed
I will bubble for you baby
I will read you some joy
We can write poetry together
I'll be for your envoys
That message in a bottle
Let you remember me as a boy
Clever girl in my head
Won't you be with me
Won't you sleep in my bed
I will bubble for you baby
It was written on the winds

It was written on the winds
How will it perpetuate baby
Tell me who wins
If we win together
      Chorus

Verse two:
I can hold clever conversations
When you're not talking to me
I can muse in a spell
Please talk to me
A clever girl in my head
Won't you be with me
Won't you sleep in my bed
I will bubble for you baby
I will read you some joy
We can write poetry together
I'll be for your envoys
That message in a bottle
Let you remember me as a boy
Clever girl in my head
Won't you be with me
Won't you sleep in my bed
I will bubble for you baby
It was written on the winds

It was written on the winds
How will it perpetuate baby
Tell me who wins
If we win together
        Chorus
                ....End song

By: Russell A. Clemo
Song Titled: **The Way Your Lips Taste**

The way your lips taste
What it does for me baby
I won't let it waste
I can't let it waste
  Chorus

  Verse one:
When I'm tasting you
Looken on your face
Fingers touching you
I'm grabben on your waist
When I'm loven you
Looken where my fingers traced
I want all of you
No feelings to base
If it's new for you
Girl take a taste
Tell me what to do
I'll give you a taste
Our bodies are natural
What is coming over you
You're acting supernatural
When it tells you what to do
Ya love is something supernatural
Now baby tell me what to do

The way your lips taste
What it does for me baby
I won't let it waste
I can't let it waste
  Chorus

Verse two:
When you're tasting me girl
Looken on my face
Fingers touchen me
You're grabben on my waist
That's when I'm loven you
Looken where your fingers traced
You want all of me
No feelings to base
If it's new for you
Girl take a taste
Tell me what to do
I'll give you a taste
Our bodies are natural
What is coming over you
You're acting supernatural
When it tells you what to do
Ya love is something supernatural
Now baby tell me what to do

The way your lips taste
What it does for me baby
I won't let it waste
I can't let it waste
Chorus
....End song

By: Russell A. Clemo
Song Titled: **If I Knew Not**

If I knew not
What I know now
Wishen I was younger
Slow it down
          Chorus

          Verse one:
I couldn't remember back when
Then you'd come around
I couldn't listen to my friends
I could only watch the trends
When you would listen
I would only pretend
Not receiving my messages
So you hit the resend
If I knew not
What I know now
Wishen I was younger
Slow it down
I can't live it all again
If I could how would it end
Baby please slow it down
Rememberen the way back when
Me and all my friends
Will you tell me how it ends

If I knew not
What I know now
Wishen I was younger
Slow it down
          Chorus

.

Verse two:
I couldn't remember back then
Tell me to tell a friend
Then what comes around
I could only watch the trend
When I would listen
I would only pretend
You're not receiving messages
So I hit the resend
If I knew not
What I know now
Wishen I was younger
Slow it down
You can live it all again
If I could how would it end
Baby please slow it down
You rememberen the way back when
Me and all my friends
Will you tell me how it ends

If I knew not
What I know now
Wishen I was younger
Slow it down
      Chorus
            ....End song

By: Russell A. Clemo
Song Titled: **She's Talken To You True**

She's talken to you true
You tell her to stay the night
She says sorry we're through
When she comes back to your bed
    Chorus

        Verse one:
Stuck in a world web
I can't answer you now
Flow until it ebb
That girl dancen in my head
Keep on comen for you
Singen all on my thread
She's talken to me true
Tell her to stay the night
She says sorry we're through
Then she comes back to my bed
She says I knew it had to be you
Tonight it had to be you
I'll give you some sweet spice
See the world through my view
What comes back to me baby
It comes back to you
I'll let your dreams be with me
Tomorrow they will come true

She's talken to you true
You tell her to stay the night
She says sorry we're through
When she comes back to your bed
    Chorus

Verse two:
If you're stuck in a world web
I can't answer you now
Flow until it ebb
That girl dancen in my head
Keep on comen for you
Singen all on my thread
She's talken to me true
Tell her to stay the night
She says sorry we're through
Then she comes back to my bed
She says I knew it had to be you
Tonight it had to be you
I'll give you some sweet spice
See the world through my view
What comes back to me baby
It comes back to you
I'll let your dreams be with mine
Tomorrow they will come true

She's talken to you true
You tell her to stay the night
She says sorry we're through
When she comes back to your bed
Chorus
....End song

By: Russell A. Clemo
Song Titled: **I'm Lost And I Can't Be Found**

I'm lost and I can't be found
I'm trapped in that city
Ya I might just drowned
Tonight we'll drink it all away
            Chorus

            Verse one:
I was fenced in
Just before I was crowned
You take it all away
And I can't be found
If I never left
If I never made a sound
How can I think this way
Why do you think this way
I'm lost and I can't be found
I'm trapped in that city
Ya I might just drowned
You tell me what to say
When I don't make a sound
The guitar when it play
The drums will try to drowned
If we're all in our heads
If we're lost and can't be found
Tonight we'll drink it all away

I'm lost and I can't be found
I'm trapped in that city
Ya I might just drowned
Tonight we'll drink it all away
            Chorus

Verse two:
If you were fenced in
Just before you were crowned
They take it all away
And you can't be found
If you never left
If you never made a sound
How can you think this way
Why do they think this way
I'm lost and I can't be found
I'm trapped in that city
Ya I might just drowned
You tell me what to say
When I don't make a sound
The guitar when it play
The drums will try to drowned
If we're all in our heads
If we're lost and can't be found
Tonight we'll drink it all away

....End song

By: Russell A. Clemo
Song Titled: **She Won't Let Me Down**

She won't let me down
Baby I'm telling you
So don't let me down
Ya tell me that you're true
    Chorus

    Verse one:
Girl when I'm beggen
I'll beg for you
If I get down on my knees
When I'm asken for you
I'll make sure we fly
This is your airplane too
We'll climb so high
So that everyone can see you
Baby I climb so high
She tell me what to do
Baby let's get high
Tell me that you're true
Look down on the city
Tell me that you're true
When we touch the ground
Everyone is looken for you
As we touch the ground
I am looken for you

She won't let me down
Baby I'm telling you
So don't let me down
Ya tell me that you're true
    Chorus

Verse two:
Girl when I'm beggen
I'll beg for you
If I get down on my knees
When I'm asken for you
I'll make sure we fly
This is your airplane too
We'll climb so high
So that everyone can see you
Baby I climb so high
She tell me what to do
Baby let's get high
Tell me that you're true
Look down on the city
Tell me that you're true
When we touch the ground
Everyone is looken for you
As we touch the ground
I am looken for you

She won't let me down
Baby I'm telling you
So don't let me down
Ya tell me that you're true
Chorus
....End song

By: Russell A. Clemo
Song Titled: **My Heart Has Gone To Ground**

My heart has gone to ground
Where does it hide
My love has gone away
Gone with it all my pride
    Chorus

    Verse one:
She left it all behind
Troubles looken for her
She can't believe it designed
She didn't read it in a book
How can she run now honey
It wasn't in her look
I won't run with her now
Troubles looken for her
The devil's in the how
My feelings have me shook
I can't be her ghost
When she's pullen away from me
I can't part the sky
I want to set her free
She's street smarts baby
If she didn't read it in a book
Ya if she's runnen now honey
It wasn't in her look

My heart has gone to ground
Where does it hide
My love has gone away
Gone with it all my pride
    Chorus

Verse two:
I left it all behind
Trouble's looken for her
I can see it designed
I didn't have to read it in a book
I can run now honey
It's written in my look
I will run with her now
While troubles looken for her
The devil's in the how
My feelings have me shook
I can't be her ghost
When she's pullen away from me
I can't part the sky
But I want to set her free
She's street smarts baby
If she didn't read it in a book
Ya if she's runnen now honey
It wasn't in her look

My heart has gone to ground
Where does it hide
My love has gone away
Gone with it all my pride
Chorus
....End song

By: Russell A. Clemo
Song Tiled: **Hang On To Your Every Word**

Hang on to your every word
You hang on to me
Oh baby can't you see
I know you can see
    Chorus

    Verse one:
When I'm maken bad decisions
You're maken bad decisions with me
When you run with me
I feel all of my divisions
Baby if you love me
You can light my candle
Place it at the mantle
I'm the man on your scene
Ya the man in your dreams
Hang on to your every word
You hang on to me
Oh baby can't you see
I know you can see
Am I strong enough for you
Baby don't walk out on me
You keep me hangen on
Ya you say you're gonna let me be
That's why you're hangen on to me

Hang On To Your Every Word
You hang on to me
Oh baby can't you see
I know you can see
    Chorus

Verse two:
When I'm maken bad decisions
You're maken bad decisions with me
I know it's real love
I feel all of my divisions
If you love me baby
You can light my candle
I know that we're playen
I know what you're sayen to me
You still keep explainen
Hang on to your every word
You hang on to me
Oh baby can't you see
I know you can see
Am I strong enough for you
Baby don't walk out on me
You keep me hangen on
Ya you say you're gonna let me be
Then why you're hangen on to me

Hang On To Your Every Word
You hang on to me
Oh baby can't you see
I know you can see
Chorus
....End song

By: Russell A. Clemo
Song Titled: **Love You More Than Anything**

Love you more than anything
Ya anything in the world
Love from your baby boy
Ya love your baby boy
    Chorus

    Verse one:
Rememberen when I was little
The things you would do
You would rub my ears
I didn't have to ask you
That's when you'd talk to me
You would tell me everything
Tell me how to be that man
That man that would go on to sing
You gave me that poetry
You gave me everything
Now I'm given it back to you
We can picture everything
Dreams they will come true
Those are things for me and you
I'm gonna take care of you momma
Ya we're gonna see it through
You know that I love you
Ya I'm your baby boy

Love you more than anything
Ya anything in the world
Love from your baby boy
Ya love your baby boy
    Chorus

Verse two:
Now I'm rememberen as an adult
The things you always do
You'd talk to my tears
I didn't have to ask you
That's when you'd talk to me
You tell me everything
Tell me how to be that man
That man that would go on to sing
You give me that poetry
You give me everything
Now I'm given it back to you
We can picture everything
Dreams they will come true
Those are things for me and you
I'm gonna take care of you momma
Ya we're gonna see it through
You know that I love you
Ya I'm your baby boy

....End song

Chapter:

A Great Book of American Songs (IX.)

Russell A. Clemo

INDEX

1. Why Do I Do The Things I Do
2. Let Me Be Where You Are
3. This Time Might Be The Last
4. If You Carried Me Baby
5. I Forget Why I Taste
6. Are You The One For Me
7. Democracy Won't Let Me Choose
8. Where Could My Baby Be
9. When Love Wins
10. Baby Free Someone

By: Russell A. Clemo
Song Titled: **Why Do I Do The Things I Do**

Why do I do the things I do
I know when I look at you
I want to give you money
You want to give me money
    Chorus

        Verse one:
All the things we see
All the things we buy
When I'm in love with you
When you make me cry
I work so hard for you
Why do I work so hard
Baby you know its true
I'm amazed at how you love me
Time always stops for you
Why do I do the things I do
I know when I look at you
I want to give you money
You want to give me money
Baby I'm a lonely man
Baby shame on me
How will I live this way
Honey this is what I've got to be

Why do I do the things I do
I know when I look at you
I want to give you money
You want to give me money
    Chorus

Verse two:
All the things we see
All the things we buy
When I'm in love with you
When you make me cry
I work so hard for you
Why do I work so hard
Baby you know its true
I'm amazed at how you love me
Time always stops for you
Why do I do the things I do
I know when I look at you
I want to give you money
You want to give me money
Baby I'm a lonely man
Baby shame on me
How will I live this way
Honey this is what I've got to be

....End song

By: Russell A. Clemo
Song Titled: **Let Me Be Where You Are**

Let me be where you are
Show me good loven
Let me hold you close
This is good loven
        Chorus

        Verse one:
Don't leave me behind
Don't let my picture fade
When I am lost
Our love is still made
Don't let me fall behind
If you're lost I'll be
I won't let you fall behind
We've only just begun
We'll move through fire
Past all the limits and fire
We'll move through that wall
I'll carry you through it all
Together we can have it all
Every scar that you claim
I'll hold your hand the same
I want you to have my name
Don't be afraid to love
Your my goddess love

Let me be where you are
Show me good loven
Let me hold you close
This is good loven
        Chorus

Verse two:
I want more until it's right
I want you for this fight
I want you in your light
Our love is still made
Don't let me fall behind
Don't walk away from me
I won't let the memory fade
We've only just begun
I want to make that home
I'll take you home
Your love is enough
Your love is enough for me
Together we can have it all
Every scar that you claim
I'll hold your hand the same
I want you to have my name
Don't be afraid to love
You're my goddess love

Let me be where you are
Show me good loven
Let me hold you close
This is good loven
        Chorus
            ....End song

By: Russell A. Clemo
Song Titled: **This Time Might Be The Last**

This time might be the last
Baby I need you to fly
I need to be free of my past
Ya this time might be the last
        Chorus

        Verse one:
Take flight with broken wings
We'll fly and live so free
I will love for you
You can help me see
I will let it all go
And you can let me be
Everything that has fallen
Ya that is for the beast
Let's make love tonight
This time might be the last
Baby I need you to fly
I need to be free of my past
Ya this time might be the last
I can't run from your passion inside
Don't want your love to leave
I don't want to feel like it died
Baby I need you to fly

This time might be the last
Baby I need you to fly
I need to be free of my past
Ya this time might be the last
        Chorus

Verse two:
Take flight with broken wings
We'll fly and live so free
I will love for you
You can help me see
I will let it all go
And you can let me be
Everything that has fallen
Ya that is for the beast
Let's make love tonight
This time might be the last
Baby I need you to fly
I need to be free of my past
Ya this time might be the last
I can't run from your passion inside
Don't want your love to leave
I don't want to feel like it died
Baby I need you to fly

This time might be the last
Baby I need you to fly
I need to be free of my past
Ya this time might be the last
Chorus
....End song

By: Russell A. Clemo
Song Tiled: **If You Carried Me Baby**

If you carried me baby
The love was all the same
If I can't see you
The love was all the same
        Chorus

        Verse one:
How did you get access
Access to my memory hard
You're peeken in on me
While you ain't looken very hard
It's so easy on me
While I'm looken very scarred
You're weighen easily on me
Seeing everything that's getten marred
But you can't tarnish my name
You can't burn out my flame
If you carried me baby
The love was all the same
If I can't see you
Then it wasn't written on my name
Don't tell me that I can't see you
There's no one left to blame
Ya if it was written on the wall
Then it's everyone's wall of shame

If you carried me baby
The love was all the same
If I can't see you
The love was all the same
        Chorus

Verse two:
How did you get access
Access to my memory hard
You're peeken in on me
While you ain't looken very hard
It's so easy on me
While I'm looken very scarred
You're weighen easily on me
Seeing everything that's getten marred
But you can't tarnish my name
You can't burn out my flame
If you carried me baby
The love was all the same
If I can't see you
Then it wasn't written on my name
Don't tell me that I can't see you
There's no one left to blame
Ya if it was written on the wall
Then it's everyone's wall of shame

....End song

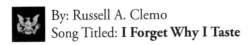 By: Russell A. Clemo
Song Titled: **I Forget Why I Taste**

I forget why I taste
I can't see her lips
I can see your wings
I can see her wing clips
        Chorus

        Verse one:
Who loaded up all the guns
Who sent us to war
What's getting pushed around
Where is the score
I can see with my gifts
I can see with how I'm blessed
How can I see honey
Now that I'm stressed
I forget why I taste
I can't see her lips
I can see your wings
I can see her wing clips
We can't fly now
I see her dirty lips
I see they're stained
Now that I am stained
She loaded up all the guns
She'll send us to war

I forget why I taste
I can't see her lips
I can see your wings
I can see her wing clips
        Chorus

Verse two:
Who loaded up all the guns
Who sent us to war
What's getting pushed around
Now you're too close to see
I can't keep going on
I can't watch you go away
Now I'm getting pushed around
Every time you go away
I forget why I taste
I can't see her lips
I can see your wings
I can see her wing clips
We can't fly now
I see her dirty lips
I see they're stained
Now that I am stained
She loaded up all the guns
She'll send us to war

....End song

By: Russell A. Clemo
Song Titled: **Are You The One For Me**

Are you the one for me
Do I want to be for you
Do you want to be free
Baby dreams do come true
          Chorus

          Verse one:
You're my reckless keeper
When I want you
It is for danger
When I don't need you
When I'm not dreamen
Ya when I sleep too
Say you're the one
You're the one for me
Say that we can make it
Leaven water underneath that bridge
Ya no wasted chances baby
You and me just liven
Girl I want to dance with you
No wasted chances given
Ya take a million pictures given
Real moments for me and you
No moments that are missen
Baby dreams do come true

Are you the one for me
Do I want to be for you
Do you want to be free
Baby dreams do come true
          Chorus

Verse two:
You're my reckless keeper
When I want you
It is for danger
When I don't need you
When I'm not dreamen
Ya when I sleep too
Say you're the one
You're the one for me
Say that we can make it
Leaven water underneath that bridge
Ya no wasted chances baby
You and me just liven
Girl I want to dance with you
No wasted chances given
Ya take a million pictures given
Real moments for me and you
No moments that are missen
Baby dreams do come true

....End song

By: Russell A. Clemo
Song Titled: **Democracy Won't Let Me Choose**

Democracy won't let me choose
Everybody tells me no
Ya baby just leave town
They tell you which way to go
    Chorus

    Verse one:
Baby don't look for me
I've just left town
Can't be with everybody
Everybody is locked down
I'm goen somewhere
Everybody tryen to lose
Governor won't let me choose
President sends him loose
Democracy won't let me choose
Everybody tells me no
Ya baby just leave town
They tell you which way to go
But they don't really know
Open up the sky for me
Let my feelings flow
Baby don't look for me
I'll get it on the run
Ya that's when I'll let go

Democracy won't let me choose
Everybody tells me no
Ya baby just leave town
They tell you which way to go
    Chorus

Verse two:
Baby don't look for me
I've just left town
Can't be with everybody
Everybody is locked down
I'm goen somewhere
Everybody tryen to lose
Governor won't let me choose
President sends him loose
Democracy won't let me choose
Everybody tells me no
Ya baby just leave town
They tell you which way to go
But they don't really know
Open up the sky for me
Let my feelings flow
Baby don't look for me
I'll get it on the run
Ya that's when I'll let go

Democracy won't let me choose
Everybody tells me no
Ya baby just leave town
They tell you which way to go
Chorus
....End song

By: Russell A. Clemo
Song Titled: **Where Could My Baby Be**

Where could my baby be
She's runnen now honey
Runnen away from me
While I can see
    Chorus

    Verse one:
I can't lose faith
I can't go crazy
In a short light maybe
But where is the dark
I know I need you baby
I need you like an arc
If I can't have you
I ain't got a spark
You can't run from me
Then I won't let you down
Ya I can't let you down
So baby please stay
I'm taken sips from my wine
I'm feeling stranded here
Ya I can't suspend in time
While I can see you runnen
I can see you breathen
Ya I can feel you inside

Where could my baby be
She's runnen now honey
Runnen away from me
While I can see
    Chorus

Verse two:
I can't lose faith
I can't go crazy
You need my light maybe
But where is the dark
You know you need me baby
You need me on that line
If I can't have you
I ain't got a sign
You can run from me
But then I can't let you down
Ya I won't let you down
So baby please stay
You're taken sips from my wine
You're feeling stranded here
Ya you can't suspend in time
While I can see you runnen
I can see you breathen
Ya I can feel you inside

Where could my baby be
She's runnen now honey
Runnen away from me
While I can see
Chorus
....End song

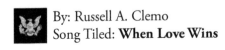 By: Russell A. Clemo
Song Tiled: **When Love Wins**

When love wins
When love frees you
We can open up our hearts
Don't leave the world behind
      Chorus

        Verse one:
We can see in the dark
We can see with a heart
Give us the answers
Ones without disaster
We are your problems
Is there a happy ever after
What of your life
Did we both ever matter
When you shine a light
Did it ever matter
What about life baby
The world in happy ever after
Many men walk the road
Many women walk the road
Going the only way they were shown
When I am with you baby
Are you with me too
Together we can see in the dark

When love wins
When love frees you
We can open up our hearts
Don't leave the world behind
      Chorus

Verse two:
We can see in the dark
We can see with a heart
Thankful for the answers
Ones without disaster
We are your problems
But there's a happy ever after
What of your life
We both always mattered
When you shine that light
I know it always mattered
Ya what about life baby
The world and happy ever after
Many men walk the road
Many women walk the road
Going the only way they were shown
When I am with you baby
I know you're with me too
Together we can see in the dark

When love wins
When love frees you
We can open up our hearts
Don't leave the world behind
Chorus
....End song

By: Russell A. Clemo
Song Titled: **Baby Free Someone**

Baby free someone
She's gonna free someone
Ya she's gonna free someone
         Chorus

         Verse one:
Keep my heart in the fight
I can feel you here
Feel you in the night
Bring it from the other side
Give me someone from the other side
Let me feel their light
When the rain is gone
When the moon is bright
Not looken through a fog
Baby free someone
She's gonna free someone
Ya she's gonna free someone
Keep your heart in the fight
You can feel me here
Feel me in the night
Bring it from the other side
Give me someone from the other side
Ya baby free someone

Baby free someone
She's gonna free someone
Ya she's gonna free someone
         Chorus

Verse two:
A heart in the fight
Your in my sights
You can see me
You can see my plight
Dreamen of a dream
Let me feel the light
Wet when it rains
Water in your light
Not looken through a fog
Baby free someone
She's gonna free someone
Ya she's gonna free someone
Another heart in the fight
You can feel me here
Feel me in the night
Bring it from the other side
Give me someone from the other side
Ya baby free someone

....End song

Chapter:

A Great Book of American Songs (X.)

Russell A. Clemo

INDEX

1. I Wrote With My Pen Today
2. Bartender You're A Friend Of Mine
3. She Will See What My Love Brings
4. God Was Good To That Woman
5. Drop The Lights Down Low
6. I Wanna Ride Free
7. I'll Be Your Tattoo Johnny
8. I Can Feel Your Heart Honey
9. Looken At A Desert Sky
10. You Held The Hand That Pulled The Trigger

By: Russell A. Clemo
Song Titled: **I Wrote With My Pen Today**

I wrote with my pen today
Talked to my other friend
I spoke for a time
I spoke to my other friend
        Chorus

        Verse one:
Watching no more waiting
No more hesitating
No more memories fading
I cant' let you slip away
Ya only for today baby
Please don't slip away
I need the queen of clubs
Or the queen of hearts
I wrote with my pen today
Talked to my other friend
I spoke for a time
I spoke to my other friend
Ya you let words live
They live just for you
Here's a drink pretty baby
A drink just for you
Talking to my other friend
That's when I talk to you

I wrote with my pen today
Talked to my other friend
I spoke for a time
I spoke to my other friend
        Chorus

Verse two:
What I see with you
No more hesitating
Grab those memories fading
Don't let me slip away
Ya only for today baby
Please don't slip away
I need the queen of clubs
Or the queen of hearts
I wrote with my pen today
Talked to my other friend
I spoke for a time
I spoke to my other friend
Ya you let words live
They live just for you
Here's another drink pretty baby
Another drink just for you
Talking to my other friend
That's when I talk to you

....End song

By: Russell A. Clemo
Song Titled: **Bartender You're A Friend Of Mine**

Bartender you're a friend of mine
I want a drink of your whiskey
I am ready to unwind
While I'm looken into my glass
You're a friend of mine
        Chorus

        Verse one:
Bartender you're a friend of mine
Sitting here with you
I ain't looken at the time
I got a friend in you
You give me a piece of your mind
Pour me another drink of some Jack
I'm tired after the long grind
Ya all day I've been worken
Now its time to unwind
Bartender you're a friend of mine
I knew I'd find you here
Ya you aint hard to find
Pour yourself a tall beer
Let me hear what's on your mind
This round is on me
The next round is too
I know I ain't gotta ask you
Bartender you're a friend of mine

Bartender you're a friend of mine
I want a drink of your whiskey
I am ready to unwind
While I'm looken into my glass
You're a friend of mine
        Chorus

Verse two:
Bartender you're a friend of mine
Sitting here with you
I ain't looken at the time
I got a friend in you
You give me a piece of your mind
Pour me another drink of some Jack
I'm tired after the long grind
Ya all day I've been worken
Now its time to unwind
Bartender you're a friend of mine
I knew I'd find you here
Ya you aint hard to find
Pour yourself a tall beer
Let me hear what's on your mind
This round is on me
The next round is too
I know I ain't gotta ask you
Bartender you're a friend of mine

....End song

By: Russell A. Clemo
Song Titled: **She Will See What My Love Brings**

She will see what my love brings
Baby tomorrow is a brand new day
Another day that I can show her
Ya see what my love brings
      Chorus

      Verse one:
She can feel the fire
The fire inside of me
She can see it baby
Standen there next to me
When she is standen there
My ambition is her ecstacy
Who can give her everything
She will see what my love brings
Baby tomorrow is a brand new day
Another day that I can show her
Ya see what my love brings
See that she can feel the fire
The fire inside of me
Make sure that she can see it
Standen there next to me
When she's standen there
Standen there next to me
She will see what my love brings

She will see what my love brings
Baby tomorrow is a brand new day
Another day that I can show her
Ya see what my love brings
      Chorus

Verse two:
Can feel the flame
The flame inside of me
She can feel it baby
Standen there next to me
When she is standen there
My ambition is her ecstacy
Who can give her everything
She will see what my love brings
Baby tomorrow is a brand new day
Another day that I can show her
Ya see what my love brings
See that she can feel the flame
The flame inside of me
Make sure that she can see it
Standen there next to me
When she's standen there
Standen there next to me
She will see what my love brings

....End song

By: Russell A. Clemo
Song Titled: **God Was Good To That Woman**

God was good to that woman
He took his time on her
Created all that magic
He took a day just for her
    Chorus

    Verse one:
A woman's beauty
Her beauty and her love
I'm so thankful honey
Ya I'm looken up above
Let me tell you about that woman
For all of her gifts
Each life that she touches
She gave me a love like this
God was good to that woman
He took his time on her
Created all that magic
He took a day just for her
I remember the day and time
When I gave her a ring
When I made her mine
Tell me is there more beauty in time
How could it be better spent
That woman was heaven sent

God was good to that woman
He took his time on her
Created all that magic
He took a day just for her
    Chorus

Verse two:
A woman's beauty
Her beauty and her love
I'm so thankful honey
Ya I'm looken up above
Let me tell you about that woman
For all of her gifts
Each life that she touches
She gave me a love like this
God was good to that woman
He took his time on her
Created all that magic
He took a day just for her
I remember the day and time
When I gave her a ring
When I made her mine
Tell me is there more beauty in time
How could it be better spent
That woman was heaven sent

God was good to that woman
He took his time on her
Created all that magic
He took a day just for her
    Chorus
            ....End song

By: Russell A. Clemo
Song Titled: **Drop The Lights Down Low**

Drop the lights down low
Show me how far to go
When I'm maken bad decisions
Ya decisions just for you
Turn them lights down low
        Chorus

        Verse one:
With the lights down low
With everything so slow
When I look around
When I look at you
I am never listening
I can't ever listen to you
Ya come now honey
Bob Dylan tells me you
Drop the lights down low
Show me how far to go
When I'm maken bad decisions
Ya decisions just for you
The cradle is in your hands
The silver spoon is in your hands
The mistakes we've made
Ya the mistakes I've made baby
We both know how its played
Just turn them lights down low

Drop the lights down low
Show me how far to go
When I'm maken bad decisions
Ya decisions just for you
Turn them lights down low
        Chorus

Verse two:
With the lights down low
With everything so slow
I can see your colors
I can feel them flow
When we are so beautiful
Ya we are so beautiful it's true
When I can listen
Bob Dylan tells me you
Drop the lights down low
Show me how far to go
When I'm maken bad decisions
Ya decisions just for you
The cradle is in your hands
The silver spoon is in your hands
The mistakes we've made
Ya the mistakes I've made baby
We both know how it's played
Just turn them lights down low

Drop the lights down low
Show me how far to go
When I'm maken bad decisions
Ya decisions just for you
Turn them lights down low
Chorus

....End song

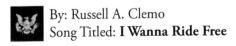 By: Russell A. Clemo
Song Titled: **I Wanna Ride Free**

I Wanna Ride Free
Free from my sin
Ride on my motorcycle
My hair in the wind
     Chorus

     Verse one:
I know how it started
I don't know how it will end
Riden as an outlaw
I know I can't pretend
When people are looken
Let em see what they like
I wanna ride free
All I can hear are my pipes
A cowboy and an outlaw
Ya I do what I like
If you wanna ride with me darlin
We can leave here tonight
Up and down the west coast
From here to Minnesota
We can take a ride honey
We'll see Sturgis South Dakota
Baby I only know how it started
I don't know how it will end

I Wanna Ride Free
Free from my sin
Ride on my motorcycle
My hair in the wind
     Chorus

Verse two:
I know how it started
I don't know how it will end
Riden as an outlaw
I know I can't pretend
When people are looken
Let em see what they like
I wanna ride free
All I can hear are my pipes
A cowboy and an outlaw
Ya I do what I like
If you wanna ride with me darlin
We can leave here tonight
Up and down the west coast
From here to Minnesota
We can take a ride honey
We'll see Sturgis South Dakota
Baby I only know how it started
I don't know how it will end

I Wanna Ride Free
Free from my sin
Ride on my motorcycle
My hair in the wind
        Chorus
                ….End song

By: Russell A. Clemo
Song Titled: **I'll Be Your Tattoo Johnny**

I'll Be Your Tattoo Johnny
You know it feels just right
Dance you around that floor
Holden your waist real tight
I'll be tattoo Johnny
       Chorus

       Verse one:
Baby you'll be my good time
You will be my love
You can be my rhyme
Don't break your baby
Can't break for my baby
You dancen keepen time
Let the dance floor fade me
I'm tryen to fly so high
You and me one night
You can be my angel
Ya we can do this right
I'll be your tattoo Johnny
You know it feels just right
Dance you around that floor
Holden your waist real tight
I'll be your tattoo Johnny
I ain't one for leaven
Ya you ain't one for leaven
I'll be yours little baby
You can be my honey bee
Lots of love from you now
Lots of love from me
We're ready to make it now
Ya honey you will see

I'll be your tattoo Johnny
You know it feels just right

Dance you around that floor
Holden your waist real tight
I'll be your tattoo Johnny
    Chorus

    Verse two:
You've always been my good time
I will be your love
You can be my rhyme
You don't want to break your baby
I cant break now baby
Now your dancen keepen time
Watch the sun faden you honey
Your tryen to fly so high
You and me tonight
You know that your my angel
Ya we can do this right
I'll be your tattoo Johnny
You know it feels just right
Dance you around that floor
Holden your waist real tight
I'll be your tattoo Johnny
You ain't one for leaven me
Ya so I ain't leaven you
I'll be yours little baby
You can be my honey bee
Lots of love for you now
Lots of love from me
We're ready to make it now
Ya honey you will see

I'll be your tattoo Johnny
You know it feels just right
Dance you around that floor
Holden your waist real tight
I'll be your tattoo Johnny
    Chorus
        ....End song

By: Russell A. Clemo
Song Titled: **I Can Feel Your Heart Honey**

I Can Feel Your Heart Honey
Ya I'm fighting for you
I can feel your heart baby
Ya I'm fighting for you
    Chorus

    Verse one:
I can see your troubles now
I'll help you get through
I'll listen to your troubles baby
While your fighting to get through
You can tell me your dreams darlin
Until there's something renewed
I can see your dreams baby
Your very foundations renewed
I can feel your heart honey
I'm fighting for you
I'll give you strength you need
Ya I'll carry you through
If you don't understand
If you can't see it too
If you need a helping hand
It'll be just me and you
Ya I'm fighting for you
I'm fighting for you

I Can Feel Your Heart Honey
Ya I'm fighting for you
I can feel your heart baby
Ya I'm fighting for you
    Chorus

Verse two:
I can see your troubles now
I'll help you get through
I'll listen to your troubles baby
While your fighting to get through
You can tell me your dreams darlin
Until there's something renewed
I can see your dreams baby
Your very foundations renewed
I can feel your heart honey
I'm fighting for you
I'll give you strength you need
Ya I'll carry you through
If you don't understand
If you can't see it too
If you need a helping hand
It'll be just me and you
Ya I'm fighting for you
I'm fighting for you

....End song

By: Russell A. Clemo
Song Titled: **Looken At A Desert Sky**

Looken at a desert sky
Orange blue pink and purple
I don't need to wonder why
It's orange blue pink and purple
    Chorus

    Verse one:
Early morning looking up at you
Early morning I prepare for two
Getting ready for the day
Getting ready for me and you
That's how I make my way
That's how I face the day
Everyday looken at a desert sky
I don't need to wonder why
I'm comen home to sugar and honey
Promise to love that woman till I die
Until God take me up into the sky
It's orange blue pink and purple
After a long day away from you
I gotta get back home to you
My baby is so true
She's the sweetest thing I ever knew
Ya I only wanna be with you
I only wanna be with you

Looken at a desert sky
Orange blue pink and purple
I don't need to wonder why
It's orange blue pink and purple
    Chorus

Verse two:
Ya I start my day
I get up and do it again
Getting ready for the day
Getting ready with my best friend
I do it just for her
That's how we make our way
Everyday looken at a desert sky
I don't need to wonder why
I'm comen home to sugar and honey
Promise to love that woman until I die
Until God take me up into the sky
It's orange blue pink and purple
After a long day away from you
I gotta get back home to you
My baby is so true
She's the sweetest thing I ever knew
Ya I only wanna be with you
I only wanna be with you

Looken at a desert sky
Orange blue pink and purple
I don't need to wonder why
It's orange blue pink and purple
        Chorus
                ....End song

By: Russell A. Clemo
Song Titled: **You Held The Hand That Pulled The Trigger**

You held the hand that pulled the trigger
Ya you fired that man's gun baby
You knew his score for him honey
Ya marched him till that man went crazy
    Chorus

    Verse one:
You held the hand that pulled the trigger
Ya then you stole his mind
You held the hand that pulled the trigger
And you ain't hard to find
I hear six strings playen in heaven
Ya and separately I hear you
Which one of us stands in hell
Baby is it me or you
Try to separate me from all that is Godly
Tell me what's a man to do
Obstructed from any helping hands
Ya what's a man to do
If no one walks away now
Ya if I didn't ask you to
Why are you holding me here baby
All those things you didn't have to do
You won't tell people to lay down their guns
Ya you won't tell it to me true

You held the hand that pulled the trigger
Ya you fired that man's gun baby
You knew his score for him honey
Ya marched him till that man went crazy
    Chorus

Verse two:
You held the hand that pulled the trigger
Ya then you stole his mind
You held the hand that pulled the trigger
And you ain't hard to find
I hear six strings playen in heaven
Ya and separately I hear you
Which one of us stands in hell
Baby is it me or you
Try to separate me from all that is Godly
Tell me what's a man to do
Obstructed from any helping hands
Ya what's a man to do
If no one walks away now
Ya if I didn't ask you to
Why are you holding me here baby
All those things you didn't have to do
You won't tell people to lay down their guns
Ya you won't tell it to me true

You held the hand that pulled the trigger
Ya you fired that man's gun baby
You knew his score for him honey
Ya marched him till that man went crazy
        Chorus
            ….End song

Chapter:

A Great Book of American Songs (XI.)

Russell A. Clemo

INDEX

1. We Can Start Another Chapter Baby
2. A Little Boy With His Daddy
3. The Love That Is Still There
4. The Columbia River Is On That Line
5. Canary Diamonds In Your Eyes
6. Your Cowgirl Boots And Cutoff Jeans
7. You Can Be My Lady
8. I'll Park My Big Red Jeep
9. I'm On McNeil Point
10. Don't Let This Bar Close

By: Russell A. Clemo
Song Titled: **We Can Start Another Chapter Baby**

We can start another chapter baby
After summer we'll watch the leaves turn
Ya come winter we'll stoke that fire
Until spring then come summer again
        Chorus

        Verse one:
Listening to the sound of your voice
Listening to your laughter
I need the sound of your voice baby
Let me hear your laughter
Let me be a part of your voice
Let me be your ever after
We can be like this forever
We can start another chapter
After summer we'll watch the leaves turn
After summer we'll have love to burn
Ya come winter we'll stoke that fire
Until spring then come summer again
I don't want this love to ever end
You and me we'll watch this world turn
You and me we've got love to burn
You see yourself with me at every turn
Ya can you see yourself being my lady
See yourself being with me baby

We can start another chapter baby
After summer we'll watch the leaves turn
Ya come winter we'll stoke that fire
Until spring then come summer again
        Chorus

Verse two:
Good feelings touch your mind
That's love that we share
Let me stoke that fire darlin
I promise to show you how much I care
Good feelings touch your heart
Honey they will find you everywhere
We can be like this forever
We can start another chapter
After summer we'll watch the leaves turn
After summer we'll have love to burn
Ya come winter we'll stoke that fire
Until spring then come summer again
I don't want this love to ever end
You and me we'll watch this world turn
You and me we've got love to burn
See yourself with me at every turn
Ya can you see yourself being my lady
See yourself being with me baby

We can start another chapter baby
After summer we'll watch the leaves turn
Ya come winter we'll stoke that fire
Until spring then come summer again
Chorus
….End song

By: Russell A. Clemo
Song Titled: **A Little Boy With His Daddy**

A little boy with his daddy
Ya the tree they're standen in
That's when that boy saw his first buck
Ya when grandpa gone to push them in
    Chorus

    Verse one:
A little boy gone deer hunting
He's hunting with his bow
Gone hunting with his daddy
He is only twelve years old
In his Gilly suit now darlin
Ya he's out in the cold
Sitting with his daddy in that tree
They're bedded down in the cold
A little boy with his pa
A little boy with his daddy
Ya the tree they're standen in
That's when that boy saw his first buck
Ya when grandpa gone to push them in
That boy made his first draw
He took down a six point buck
Ya talken about a little boys luck
That's when he killed his first buck
They'll be talken all over town

A little boy with his daddy
Ya the tree they're standen in
That's when that boy saw his first buck
Ya when grandpa gone to push them in
    Chorus

Verse two:
A little boy gone deer hunting
He's hunting with his bow
Gone hunting with his daddy
He is only twelve years old
In his Gilly suit now darlin
Ya he's out in the cold
Sitting with his daddy in that tree
They're bedded down in the cold
A little boy with his pa
A little boy with his daddy
Ya the tree they're standen in
That's when that boy saw his first buck
Ya when grandpa gone to push them in
That boy made his first draw
He took down a six point buck
Ya talken about a little boys luck
That's when he killed his first buck
They'll be talken all over town

A little boy with his daddy
Ya the tree they're standen in
That's when that boy saw his first buck
Ya when grandpa gone to push them in
Chorus
....End song

By: Russell A. Clemo
Song Titled: **The Love That Is Still There**

The love that is still there
I know how much you care
The love that is still there
Ya I know how much you care
  Chorus

  Verse one:
The Love that is still there
All the years gone by honey
The years that we shared
I remember back in the beginning
Like it was just back there
Our yesterdays looken back
I know how much you care
Now all these years later
We're no worse for the wear
A few wrinkles around the eyes
That's something that we share
No wrinkles to iron out baby
Ya life seems pretty fair
Our children are all grown
They're all running around out there
This is a great big world
A world that we share
The Love that is still there.

The love that is still there
I know how much you care
The love that is still there
Ya I know how much you care
  Chorus

Verse two:
The Love that is still there
All the years gone by honey
We've traveled everywhere
Doesn't it seem funny
A world that we share
A world without money
We're no worse for the wear
Our children are all grown
They're all running around out there
A few wrinkles around the eyes
That's something that we share
No wrinkles to iron out baby
Ya life seems pretty fair
Our children are all grown
Our house is a loving home
Our love's without a care
A world that we share
The Love that is still there.

....End song

By: Russell A. Clemo
Song Titled: **The Columbia River Is On That Line**

The Columbia River is on that line
Ya plenty of fishen we'll drink tonight
Sitten on that water it feels just right
Baby early mornings catch me a bite
    Chorus

    Verse one:
Putten croppy on that weighted line
Ya haven us a fish fry tonight
Budlight with some beer batter baby
Cooken sturgeon fry it up just right
Toolen around in that Johnson boat
Ya sometimes until it's last light
We drop anchor and let it float
Ya until there ain't a trouble in sight
Fishen line hangen off that boat
Ya that sun it's still burnen bright
I got my trucker hat on baby
Ya my cowboy boots on tight
Let your baby get his fishen on
Ya your baby feelen just right
You can circle that boat around honey
I got two more spots in my sights
Love when the sun hits that water
The sun changes that water's light
Honey find me some water
Ya I'll stay fishen till come the night

The Columbia River is on that line
Ya plenty of fishen we'll drink tonight
Sitten on that water it feels just right
Baby early mornings catch me a bite
    Chorus

Verse two:
Putten croppy on that weighted line
Ya haven us a fish fry tonight
Budlight with some beer batter baby
Cooken sturgeon fry it up just right
Toolen around in that Johnson boat
Ya sometimes until it's last light
We drop anchor and let it float
Ya until there ain't a trouble in sight
Fishen line hangen off the boat
Ya that sun it's still burnen bright
I got my trucker hat on baby
Ya my cowboy boots on tight
Let your baby get his fishen on
Ya your baby feelen just right
You can circle that boat around honey
I got two more spots in my sights
Love when the sun hits that water
The sun changes that water's light
Honey find me some water
Ya I'll stay fishen till come the night

The Columbia River is on that line
Ya plenty of fishen we'll drink tonight
Sitten on that water it feels just right
Baby early mornings catch me a bite
        Chorus
            ....End song

By: Russell A. Clemo
Song Titled: **Canary Diamonds In Your Eyes**

Canary diamonds in your eyes
I can see them sparkle now
I see the sparkle in your eyes
Ya it is in your eyes
        Chorus

        Verse one:
Take my broken wings baby
I'll fly on broken wings
My heart is yours
My heart when it sings
Ya when it comes and goes
When I'm letting go
I can feel you close
What are you sayen to me
When I don't already know
If your heart is playen me
Won't you show me now
Canary diamonds in your eyes
I can see them sparkle now
I see the sparkle in your eyes
Ya it's in your eyes
My heart is always playen
I'm dancing for you baby
Ya you know it's true

Canary diamonds in your eyes
I can see them sparkle now
I see the sparkle in your eyes
Ya it is in your eyes
        Chorus

Verse two:
Take my broken wings baby
I'll fly on broken wings
My heart is yours
My heart when it sings
Ya when it comes and goes
When I'm letting go
I can feel you close
What are you sayen to me
When I don't already know
If your heart is playen me
Won't you show me now
Canary diamonds in your eyes
I can see them sparkle now
I see the sparkle in your eyes
Ya it's in your eyes
My heart is always playen
I'm dancing for you baby
Ya you know it's true

Canary diamonds in your eyes
I can see them sparkle now
I see the sparkle in your eyes
Ya it is in your eyes
        Chorus
            ....End song

By: Russell A. Clemo
Song Titled: **Your Cowgirl Boots And Cutoff Jeans**

Your cowgirl boots and cutoff jeans
Ya tonight it feels just right
Winden up on the radio
Let's shotgun a beer tonight
        Chorus

        Verse one:
You're beautiful standen there
The music's playen just right
Won't you dance with me baby
The campfire it's burnen so bright
Tonight you're everything that I've got
Ya baby it feels just right
Cowgirl your looken so fine
Come here baby and kiss me tonight
You and me let's shotgun a beer darlin
We'll keep dancen until first light
You want we can look at the stars
Gazen up from my truck bed tonight
Ya we do it around a campfire baby
Keep the campfire blazen bright
Your body winden up on that radio
Your hips dancen in the fire's light
Your hips are winding up darlin
Ain't gonna find my way back home tonight

Your cowgirl boots and cutoff jeans
Ya tonight it feels just right
Winden up on the radio
Let's shotgun a beer tonight
        Chorus

Verse two:
You're beautiful standen there
The music's playen just right
Won't you dance with me baby
The campfire it's burnen so bright
Tonight you're everything that I've got
Ya baby it feels just right
Cowgirl your looken so fine
Come here baby and kiss me tonight
You and me let's shotgun a beer darlin
We'll keep dancen until first light
You want we can look at the stars
Gazen up from my truck bed tonight
Ya we do it around a campfire baby
Keep the campfire blazen bright
Your body winden up on that radio
Your hips dancen in the fire's light
Your hips are winding up darlin
Ain't gonna find my way back home tonight

Your cowgirl boots and cutoff jeans
Ya tonight it feels just right
Winden up on the radio
Let's shotgun a beer tonight
         Chorus
              ....End song

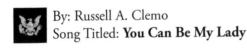 By: Russell A. Clemo
Song Titled: **You Can Be My Lady**

You can be my lady
You can remember me when honey
Ya you can be my lady
We have our look way back then
    Chorus

    Verse one:
We'll give love one more chance
We'll kiss each others lips
We'll have one more dance
We can make it like this
We can make it under pressure
More than a feeling in a kiss
Ya you're a love like this
We can gamble under pressure
I need your love like this
You can be my lady baby
Ya you remember me back when
We can't make our way back there again
Now that we're no longer younger
Now that you're a lady I can't pretend
You better miss me when I'm gone
When I leave only to come back again
When I come back now baby
No I don't want to find you gone

You can be my lady
You can remember me when honey
Ya you can be my lady
We have our look way back then
    Chorus

Verse two:
Please give love one more chance
I would kiss your lips
We'll have just one more dance
You can make it like this
You can make it under pressure
It's more than a feeling baby
You're a crazy love like this
Where is the gamble under pressure
I need your love like this
You can be my lady baby
Ya you remember me back when
We can't make our way back there again
Now that we're no longer younger
Now that you're a lady I can't pretend
You better miss me when I'm gone
When I leave only to come back again
When I come back now baby
No I don't want to find you gone

You can be my lady
You can remember me when honey
Ya you can be my lady
We have our look way back then
        Chorus
            ….End song

By: Russell A. Clemo
Song Titled: **I'll Park My Big Red Jeep**

I'll park my big red jeep
Right where the sand and pavement meets
It's you and me honey baby
We'll climb out of those bucket seats
    Chorus

    Verse one:
Take the hardtop off of my Jeep
A pair of sandals on my feet
My board shorts on baby
Ya I won't miss a beat
You and me let's find a beach
Ya I'll park my big red jeep
Right where the sand and pavement meets
It's you and me honey baby
We'll climb out of those bucket seats
Find a spot nice and sunny
We can spend our summer like that
You with your bikini and your beach hat
I love to watch you tan baby
Ya honey it's just like that
We're chasen daylight with some cold beer
Brought a lime squeeze for you honey
Let me grab you another beer
Summer time it feels just right
You and me little darlin
Underneath the suns white light
We'll stay until the sun goes down
We're right on top of that river
Ya just on the edge of town
Just on the edge of town

I'll park my big red jeep
Right where the sand and pavement meets
It's you and me honey baby
We'll climb out of those bucket seats
     Chorus

     Verse two:
Take the hardtop off of my Jeep
A pair of sandals on my feet
My board shorts on baby
Ya I won't miss a beat
You and me let's find a beach
Ya I'll park my big red jeep
Right where the sand and pavement meets
It's you and me honey baby
We'll climb out of those bucket seats
Find a spot nice and sunny
We can spend our summer like that
You with your bikini and your beach hat
I love to watch you tan baby
Ya honey it's just like that
We're chasen daylight with some cold beer
Brought a lime squeeze for you honey
Let me grab you another beer
Summer time it feels just right
You and me little darlin
Underneath the suns white light
We'll stay until the sun goes down
We're right on top of that river
Ya just on the edge of town
Just on the edge of town

     ....End song

By: Russell A. Clemo
Song Titled: **I'm On McNeil Point**

I'm On McNeil Point
That's on Mt. Hood
There's snow on the mountain
There's a valley of good
    Chorus

    Verse one:
There's the smell of pine
I can see an eagle in the sky
The sun is shinen now
I know this feelen won't ever die
I'm on top of a mountain
I'm feeling so high
That's when I screamed
I screamed God bless America
Watchen that eagle in the sky
There's the smell of pine
Woods all around baby
There's plenty of mother nature
Everything that's on the ground
There's plenty woodland creatures
You can hear the sound
Ya hear the wolf cry
While he's looken around
You can hear the sound

I'm On McNeil Point
That's on Mt. Hood
There's snow on the mountain
There's a valley of good
    Chorus

Verse two:
There's a smell of fresh air
There's a beautiful sky
The sun is shinen
I looked an eagle in his eye
I'm on top of a mountain
I'm feeling so high
That's when I screamed
I screamed God bless America
Watchen that eagle in the sky
There's the smell of fresh air
Woods all around baby
There's plenty of mother nature
Everything that's on the ground
There's beautiful woodland creatures
You can hear the sound
Ya hear the wolf cry
Don't let it drowned
You can hear the sound

I'm On McNeil Point
That's on Mt. Hood
There's snow on the mountain
There's a valley of good
        Chorus
            ....End song

By: Russell A. Clemo
Song Titled: **Don't Let This Bar Close**

Don't let this bar close
After hours if it close
The parking lot when it goes
When will it end nobody knows
        Chorus

        Verse one:
It's a party long after close
Tailgaten outside the bar
In a small town who really knows
Ya nobody to stop us
That fun it still flows
Drinken whiskey from a bottle
Ya that beer it still flows
We keep the music playen honey
Sometimes the party only grows
No taxi to take me home
Now baby I'm drinken all night long
Music comen from a jacked up truck
Baby don't let this bar close
After hours when it close
Ya the parking lot when it goes
When will it end ya nobody knows
Little darlin holden me close
Maybe I wanna drink from her lips
That's when I get a whiskey kiss
Ya I need a few more nights like this
Come here baby and hold me close
Pass the whiskey bottle in that circle
Ya now we're maken the most
Don't let this bar close

Don't let this bar close
After hours if it close
The parking lot when it goes
When will it end nobody knows
    Chorus

    Verse two:
It's a party long after close
Tailgaten outside the bar
In a small town who really knows
Ya nobody to stop us
That fun it still flows
Drinken whiskey from a bottle
Ya that beer it still flows
We keep the music playen honey
Sometimes the party only grows
No taxi to take me home
Now baby I'm drinken all night long
Music comen from a jacked up truck
Baby don't let this bar close
After hours when it close
Ya the parking lot when it goes
When will it end ya nobody knows
Little darlin holden me close
Maybe I wanna drink from her lips
That's when I get a whiskey kiss
Ya I need a few more nights like this
Come here baby and hold me close
Pass the whiskey bottle in that circle
Ya now we're maken the most
Don't let this bar close

    ....End song

Chapter:

A Great Book of American Songs (XII.)

Russell A. Clemo

INDEX

1. Down Every Road You Traveled
2. When We're Maken Love
3. Two Will Fight Over You
4. Out In The City Light
5. Life Is A Raincheck
6. I'm Feeling Different Levels In Paradise
7. Live For Me If You Can
8. You Taste From The Rains
9. You're That Small Town Girl
10. I'm Taken My Show To Tennessee

By: Russell A. Clemo
Song Titled: **Down Every Road You Traveled**

Down every road you traveled
Travel along with you
Everywhere that you went
I was there with you
    Chorus

    Verse one:
Whenever you fly away
I take to wing with you
When you return
I am yours so true
There from the beginning
When you were so young
As you got older too
We were haven fun
It was always you
Down every road you traveled
Travel along with you
Everywhere you went
I was their with you
No danger in your wings
Nothing to worry you
In love with a singing man
Ya what do you do

Down every road you traveled
Travel along with you
Everywhere that you went
I was there with you
    Chorus

Verse two:
Whenever you fly away
I take to wing with you
When you return
I am yours so true
There from the beginning
When you were so young
As you got older too
We were haven fun
It was always you
Down every road you traveled
Travel along with you
Everywhere you went
I was their with you
No danger in your wings
Nothing to worry you
In love with a singing man
Ya what do you do

Down every road you traveled
Travel along with you
Everywhere that you went
I was there with you
Chorus
....End song

By: Russell A. Clemo
Song Titled: **When We're Maken Love**

When we're maken love
You're given your love
I'm maken love baby
I'm maken love for you
    Chorus

    Verse one:
I'm naked under the moon
Naked in the night
On a city roof top
The stars burning bright
Ya out of the light
She says it's all in her head
Ya she's all in my head
She's naked under the moon
When we're maken love
You're given your love
I'm maken love baby
I'm maken love for you
Under that talking city light
A naked body burnen bright
Our beautiful city roof top
Both naked in the night
Let the love be our flame
While we're naked in the night

When we're maken love
You're given your love
I'm maken love baby
I'm maken love for you
    Chorus

Verse two:
You're naked under the moon
Ya naked in the night
We're on a city roof top
The stars burning bright
Ya dancen in the light
Ya you're all in my head
A goddess naked under the moon
Baby now we're maken love
You're given it underneath the moon
I'm maken love baby
I'm maken love for you
Under that talking city light
A naked body burning bright
Our beautiful city roof top
Both naked in the night
Let the love be our flame
While we're naked in the night
When we're maken love

....End song

By: Russell A. Clemo
Song Titled: **Two Will Fight Over You**

Two will fight over you
Two inside of my shoes
You can't really side
What will you do
        Chorus

        Verse one:
Underneath of a cloud
Inside of some rain
If you're in a deluge
You can see my pain
Will you reach out
Baby reach out for me
I'm only a temporary touch
When inside you're not free
Ya I'll try to set you free
Two will fight over you
Two inside of my shoes
You can't really side
What will you do
Try to run away with me
Everyone will follow us
Inside you can see
Don't stand underneath a cloud
Inside of some rain

Two will fight over you
Two inside of my shoes
You can't really side
What will you do
        Chorus

Verse two:
Underneath of that cloud
Inside of that rain
If you're in a deluge
You can see my pain
I will reach out
So reach out for me
I'm only a temporary touch
When inside I'm not free
Ya I'll try to set you free
Two will fight over you
Two inside of my shoes
You can't really side
What will you do
Try to run away with me
Everyone will follow us
Inside you can see
Don't stand underneath a cloud
Inside of some rain

Two will fight over you
Two inside of my shoes
You can't really side
What will you do
        Chorus
                ....End song

By: Russell A. Clemo
Song Titled: **Out In The City Light**

Out in the city light
Two angels in the night
Ya in a California light
Baby we can make it tonight
        Chorus

        Verse one:
I'll tear my heart out
Tryen to cleanse my heart
I'll tear my wings
Tryen to fly me home
Ya I can't find my way home
I want to love you baby
Like I'm going to lose you
Baby you love me too
So don't let me lose you
Out in the city light
Two angels in the night
Ya in a California light
Baby we can make it tonight
You can fly me home
You said if I'm dreamen tonight
No more dreamen tonight
Dreamen about you and me
Ya dreamen until we're free

Out in the city light
Two angels in the night
Ya in a California light
Baby we can make it tonight
        Chorus

Verse two:
You can tear my heart out
Baby tryen to cleanse my heart
You'll tear my wings
Tryen to fly me on home
Ya when I can't find my way home
I want to love you baby
Like I'm going to lose you
Baby you love me too
So don't let me lose you
You're out in the city light
Two angels in the night
Ya we're in a California light
Baby we can make it tonight
I can fly you home
You said if I'm dreamen tonight
No more dreamen tonight
Dreamen about you and me
Ya dreamen until we're free

Out in the city light
Two angels in the night
Ya in a California light
Baby we can make it tonight
     Chorus
         ….End song

By: Russell A. Clemo
Song Titled: **Life Is A Raincheck**

Life is a raincheck
When life isn't through yet
But ya it's a safe bet
Because I'm already through yet
　　　Chorus

　　　Verse one:
Ya life is a raincheck
When life isn't so lonely
You're not through yet
If something is so phony
Honey you are not alone
Ya you got your friends
Home's inside of your head now
Wishen you were alive now
How could we figure it out
Ya we're so alive now
When they helped you figure it out
Some people almost died now
We pull together with welcoming hands
When life is a raincheck
When you're life isn't through yet
Stay inside if your still wet
Who are we little baby
Ya life isn't through yet

Life is a raincheck
When life isn't through yet
But ya it's a safe bet
Because I'm already through yet
　　　Chorus

Verse two:
Ya I'm on the other side
I'm on the other side
Your love with your pride
Where can loneliness wait
We won't let it hide
Ya you got your friends
Home's inside of your head now
Wishen you were alive now
How could we figure it out
Ya we're so alive now
When everyone else helped you figure it out
Some people almost died now
We pull together with welcoming hands
When your life is a raincheck
When your life isn't through yet
Stay inside if that window's wet
Who are we little baby
Ya life isn't through yet

....End song

By: Russell A. Clemo
Song Titled: **I'm Feeling Different Levels In Paradise**

I'm feeling different levels in Paradise
I can paint these pictures
I can see through these eyes
I'm feeling different levels in Paradise
    Chorus

        Verse one:
I'm feelen different levels
You can call it wise
Everyone looken at the future
Not looken for my prize
I ain't worken harder for you
I've been cut to my size
If I'm a diamond for you
I can see through those eyes
If I'm a diamond for you baby
I'm feeling different levels in Paradise
I can paint these pictures
I can see through these eyes
I'm feeling different levels in Paradise
The sum of all my highs for you
If everyone is so true
They're getting high for you too
Ya I will revel for you darlin
Baby I will revel for you

I'm feeling different levels in Paradise
I can paint these pictures
I can see through these eyes
I'm feeling different levels in Paradise
    Chorus

Verse two:
You're feeling different levels
I can call it wise
Everyone looken at the future
Not looken for your prize
You ain't worken harder for me
You've been cut to your size
If you're a diamond for me
I can see through those eyes
If you're a diamond for me baby
I'm feeling different levels in Paradise
I can paint these pictures
I can see through these eyes
I'm feeling different levels in Paradise
The sum of all my highs for you
If everyone is so true
They're getting high for you too
Ya I will revel for you darlin
Baby I will revel for you

I'm feeling different levels in Paradise
I can paint these pictures
I can see through these eyes
I'm feeling different levels in Paradise
Chorus
....End song

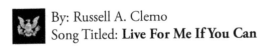 By: Russell A. Clemo
Song Titled: **Live For Me If You Can**

Live for me if you can
Do what you will honey
I will be for you
I will be your man
          Chorus

          Verse one:
You don't need to worry
I will help you now
Come to me little baby
Ya please don't worry now
I'm not hiding from the clouds
No trouble when I see rain
I can see so clearly now
I don't feel any pain
I still look to the sky in wonderment
Looking for a higher plane
But it's your love I feel now
Can we do it all again
Live for me if you can
Do what you will honey
I will be for you
I will be your man
If we come back together
I will help you now
Even when you hear thunder
There is lightening happening now
Baby don't hide from the clouds
What's welcome in the night
I want to feel you here
I want to feel you in my light

Live for me if you can
Do what you will honey

I will be for you
I will be your man
    Chorus

    Verse two:
The world will always worry
Who will help us now
What comes to me in a dream
I don't worry now
I'm not hiding from the clouds
No trouble when I see rain
You can see so clearly now
And you can't see my pain
When I'm looking to the sky
Looking for a higher plane
All I want is your love now
We can do it all again
Live for me if you can
Do what you will honey
I will be for you
I will be your man
When we come back together
You can help me now
Even when you hear thunder
There is lightening happening now
Baby don't hide from the clouds
Everything's welcome in the night
I want to feel you here
I want to feel you in my light

Live for me if you can
Do what you will honey
I will be for you
I will be your man
    Chorus
        ….End song

By: Russell A. Clemo
Song Tiled: **You Taste From The Rains**

You taste from the rains
You break away from your chains
Moments you've already lived before
Ya honey you are what remains
  Chorus

  Verse one:
If you live for today
Worry about tomorrow baby
Not thinking about yesterday
What is that consumes you
It's waiting for you in yesterday
I'll help you walk away
I'll show you the way
It's inside of a light
Ya honey there is a way
You taste from the rains
You break away from your chains
Moments you've already lived before
Ya honey you are what remains
Stuck inside of that loop
You're a circle of life
You want things to be different
You want to see it right
You taste from the rains

You taste from the rains
You break away from your chains
Moments you've already lived before
Ya honey you are what remains
  Chorus

Verse two:
If I live for today
I'll worry about tomorrow baby
I'm not thinken about yesterday
What is that consumes me
It's waiting for me in yesterday
I'll help you walk away
I'll show you the way
It's inside of a light
Ya honey there is a way
You taste from the rains
You break away from your chains
Moments you've already lived before
Ya honey you are what remains
I'll walk away with you
We'll leave here tonight
Under all of that city light
We'll be burning so bright
You taste from the rains

You taste from the rains
You break away from your chains
Moments you've already lived before
Ya honey you are what remains
        Chorus
            ....End song

By: Russell A. Clemo
Song Titled: **You're That Small Town Girl**

You're that small town girl
Small town girl that's free
I want you to dance for me
Ya girl you're so wild and free
        Chorus

        Verse one:
We'll dance in the firelight
We can do it all night
Baby it's just you and me
You're my jewel you're my baby
Girl you know anyone can see
You're my girl you're my lady
Ya under the moonlight we can see
Together it's just you and me
Ya you're my best friend
You're that small town girl
Ya small town girl that's free
Baby I want you to dance for me
Ya girl you're so wild and free
You can dance for me
Small town girl that's free
Ya you're the Bonnie to my Clyde
In a jacked up truck we're free
Ya in that jacked up truck we're free

You're that small town girl
Small town girl that's free
I want you to dance for me
Ya girl you're so wild and free
        Chorus

Verse two:
We'll dance by the headlights
Girl we can do it all night
Honey its just you and me
You're my jewel you're my baby
You're given me love and some ecstacy
You're my girl you're my lady
Ya under the moonlight we can see
Together it's just you and me
Ya you're my best friend
You're that small town girl
Ya small town girl that's free
Baby I want you to dance for me
Ya girl you're so wild and free
You can dance for me
Small town girl that's free
Ya you're the Bonnie to my Clyde
In a jacked up truck we're free
Ya in that jacked up truck we're free

....End song

By: Russell A. Clemo
Song Titled: **I'm Taken My Show To Tennessee**

I'm taken my show to Tennessee
I'm tryen to take my show to you
When I'm maken music baby
I do it just for you
        Chorus

        Verse one:
I knew from the last time
Knew with not a crime
I can see you true
Don't need all of the shine
I just want my baby
Just want my time
I just want you honey
Ya I know it's my time
You know I do what it does
I'm taken my show to Tennessee
I'm tryen to take my show to you
When I'm maken music baby
I do it just for you
One trip around the world
Ya one trip with you
The first stop & the last stop
So that I'm comen back to you
Ya I'm comen back to you

I'm taken my show to Tennessee
I'm tryen to take my show to you
When I'm maken music baby
I do it just for you
        Chorus

Verse two:
You knew from the last time
Knew with not a crime
You can see you're true
Don't need all of the shine
You know you want me too
You always want my time
I just want you honey
Ya I know it's my time
You know I do what it does
I'm taken my show to Tennessee
I'm tryen to take my show to you
When I'm maken music baby
I do it just for you
One trip around the world
Ya one trip with you
The first stop & the last stop
So that I'm comen back to you
Ya I'm comen back to you

I'm taken my show to Tennessee
I'm tryen to take my show to you
When I'm maken music baby
I do it just for you
Chorus
....End song

Printed in the USA
CPSIA information can be obtained
at www.ICGtesting.com
LVHW011554020424
775992LV00014B/170